"In *The Colors of Hope*, Richard Dahlstrom brings a welcome call to a biblical faith that calls us beyond ourselves and the polarized debates in our society. He invites us to discover the unique ways God can use our lives and paintbrushes to bring the colors of compassion, justice, and celebration to a world hungry to find a little hope. We in Seattle are glad to share Richard Dahlstrom's prophetic voice with Christians throughout our society who want to take Scripture seriously in their lives, churches, and in our troubled world."

—Tom Sine (www.msainfo.org)
Author, *The New Conspirators: Creating the Future One Mustard Seed at a Time*

"Revolutions begin among artists—our poets, painters, storytellers, and musicians. *The Colors of Hope* marks Richard Dahlstrom as a revolutionary. Passionately, deftly, Dahlstrom urges us to embrace our calling as artisans of hope. This is the soothing voice and the relevant message that this noisy, weary world needs."

—Karen Spears Zacharias
Author, *Will Jesus Buy Me a Double-Wide? 'cause I need more room for my plasma TV* (Zondervan)

"If we truly believe in the resurrection of Christ, we believe in this good news not only for the annual Easter weekend, but we believe that God has risen and is at work *every* day. But more important, we choose not to be bystanders but to be active participants in God's redemptive work. This is what this compelling book is all about. Richard Dahlstrom reminds us that cynicism and hopelessness are not going to change the world. But neither will nebulous idealism. We have to become people of mercy, justice, and love. In short, we have to be 'artisans of hope.' "

—Eugene Cho
Pastor and Founder, One Day's Wages

"Anyone who's followed Jesus for a while has seen gray areas, when vibrant faith fades into the drudgery of religion. Richard Dahlstrom, one of the brightest and best communicators Christianity has to offer right now, calls us out into fulfilling our role as creators; artists sent to splash the world with meaningful, gorgeous color. It's a lot better than moping around waiting for Armageddon."

—Jordan Green
  Director, Burnside Writers Collective
  (www.burnsidewriters.com)

THE
COLORS
OF HOPE

BECOMING PEOPLE
of MERCY, JUSTICE,
AND LOVE

Richard Dahlstrom

BakerBooks

a division of Baker Publishing Group
Grand Rapids, Michigan

Published by Baker Books
a division of Baker Publishing Group
P.O. Box 6287, Grand Rapids, Michigan.
www.bakerbooks.com
Printed in the United States of America

Library of Congress Cataloging-in-Publication Data
Dahlstrom, Richard, 1956–   .
   The colors of hope : becoming people of mercy, justice, and love / Richard Dahlstrom.
      p.   cm.
   Includes bibliographical references.
   ISBN 978-0-8010-1356-0 (pbk. : alk. paper)   1. Christian life.   2. Service (Theology).   3. Hope—Religious aspects—Christianity.   I. Title.
   BV4520.D34   2011
   248.4—dc22   2011002288

Unless otherwise identified, Scripture quotations are taken from the NEW AMERICAN STANDARD BIBLE,® Copyright © The Lockman Foundation 1960, 1962, 1963, 1968, 1971, 1972, 1973, 1975, 1977, 1995 by International Bible Society. Used by permission. (www.Lockman.org)

Scripture quotations identified ESV are from The Holy Bible, English Standard Version, copyright © 2001 by Crossway Bibles, a division of Good News Publishers. Used by permission. All rights reserved.

Scripture quotations identified GW are from GOD'S WORD,® © 1995 by God's Word to the Nations. Used by permission of Baker Publishing Group. All rights reserved.

Scripture quotations identified KJV are from the King James Version of the Bible.

Scripture quotations identified THE MESSAGE are from The Message. Copyright © 1993, 1994, 1995 by Eugene H. Peterson. Used by permission of NavPress Publishing Group.

Scripture quotations identified NIV are from the Holy Bible, New International Version.® Copyright © 1973, 1978, 1984 by Biblica, Inc.™ Used by permission of Zondervan. All rights reserved worldwide. www.zondervan.com.

Scripture quotations identified NKJV are from the New King James Version of the Bible. Copyright © 1979, 1980, 1982 by Thomas Nelson, Inc. Used by permission. All rights reserved.

Scripture quotations identified NLT are from the Holy Bible, New Living Translation, copyright © 1996, 2004. Used by permission of Tyndale House Publishers, Inc., Wheaton, Illinois 60189. All rights reserved.

DEDICATION

Our world is filled with people who are, anonymously and without accolade, bringing food to the hungry, water to the thirsty, hospitality and shelter to the stranger, education to the ignorant, healing to the sick, justice to the oppressed, protection to the vulnerable, clothing to the naked, hope to the hopeless, all in Jesus' name. Thank you for painting the colors of hope so lavishly, vividly, faithfully. This book is dedicated to you.

ACKNOWLEDGMENTS

This work wouldn't be possible without my artist friends. They shake me awake, opening my eyes to beauty, tragedy, and possibilities in God's world. Thanks to Bryan Gough and Juliette Aristides for the studio tours, manuscript feedback, and discussions about beauty, hope, meaning, and faith. If souls are fed by friendship, I've known moments of feasting with each of you.

Because my writing happens in life's margins, my wife is behind every word. She's the one who expands my margins by absorbing life's details so that I can write. Donna, I'm blessed beyond words by the treasure of your love and friendship. Thank you.

CONTENTS

INTRODUCTION

On Becoming Artisans of Hope

Have you ever seen *Schindler's List*? Steven Spielberg's masterful film about the holocaust and the role Oskar Schindler played in saving the lives of Jews is forever etched in my mind as one of the great films of modern time. I say this because of the power of its message, the skill of its cast, and the artistry of its cinematography. Regarding the latter, one scene stands out as remarkably powerful.

Perhaps you remember it. The whole film is shot in black and white, in stark contrast to the few seconds near the middle of the movie where our eye is drawn to a small child, an individual, walking with the mass of humanity as they're forced from the Warsaw ghetto. She's in color; wearing red, she highlights the reality that though we're talking about "the Jews," we're really talking about people, because what are "the masses" other than gathered individual lives, each with a story, longings, desires, and fears? She stands out against all the shades of grey that are the rest of the world: grey streets, grey buildings, grey people, grey sky. Without any words being spoken, she embodies innocence, beauty, simplicity, and all that is good and right. She, the incarnation of hope, is where your eye is drawn.

That's as it should be. We're looking, all of us are, for hope, because God knows despair is easy enough to find without any looking at all. We run into it everywhere. We wake up to the morning news and hear about the price of oil and the threat of terrorism, pandemic, or financial scandal. Soon we're off to work, if we still have a job in the midst of the economic insanity that marks our time, wondering if our company or product is helping to make the world a better place, wondering if we're going to remain competitive what with the latest outsourcing to some farther corner of the world, because it's become too expensive to do business in China. We'll arrive home and there too, for many, *grey* might still prevail. Relational struggles, addictions, loneliness, weariness, physical afflictions, and boredom are all on the list—various shades of grey that dampen hope.

Of course, it's not all grey and certainly not all the time. There's football on Sundays, time with the kids, good moments with our spouse, a meal with friends, our workout at the gym, or even some entertainment on cable. Stirring worship or a compelling conference occasionally cheers or inspires us as well, perhaps. But for those wondering whether there's any lasting source of satisfaction, any way to make our lives count for something, any way to find real joy, the color grey still bleeds back onto the canvas of our lives inexorably, leaving us with a sense of longing. "Is this all there is?" we ask.

It's a time-honored question, asked in movies from every generation: *The Graduate* for mine, *Garden State* for my son's. The issue is pondered in lyrics like Dave Matthews' "Grey Street" and addressed by poets from every century.

Keep going further back, and you'll find one called "The Preacher" asking and then answering the same question in one of the most quoted books of the Bible, Ecclesiastes. The

Preacher, though, plays his hand at the beginning of his writings, when he says,

> Smoke, nothing but smoke.
> There's nothing to anything—it's all smoke.
> What's there to show for a lifetime of work,
> a lifetime of working your fingers to the bone?[1]

It's a rhetorical question, of course. The answer is that nothing lasts; nothing offers a sense of completion. "Like grabbing smoke," we're told.

You open your hand. And it's empty. The Preacher goes from generalization to the particulars and, in so doing, deconstructs the main narratives that have occupied humans for all time, right up to this very moment.

Money, pleasure, education, and work are the main targets of the Preacher's consideration, and in every case the conclusion is the same: we'll never be satisfied fully by any of these things. This isn't to say these things don't have value. In the right context, for the right reasons, they're gifts to be enjoyed, assets to be stewarded. But lasting satisfaction? The Preacher doesn't think so, and neither do I. They are, on their own, just not adequate to deliver the goods.

THE DISAPPOINTMENT OF RELIGION

In response to the greying that comes from our various pursuits, every generation has had its share of people who've come to be characterized by a fixation on the hopelessness of these endeavors. Their response, in various forms, has been a call to drop out of all this and "get religion."

In its basest forms, religion is a transaction between some god and some person or people group, whereby god offers a colorful afterlife in exchange for obedience and sacrifice here in this present, already grey world. Christianity isn't immune to this aberrant view, as church history and present church politics and policies remind us.

Where this form of Christianity holds sway, people of faith are characterized more by what they are against (swearing, smoking, tattoos, wearing makeup, listening to anything other than approved music, reading the wrong version of the Bible, watching movies, holding hands before being engaged, and so much more . . . it's a long and varied list, depending on the century and geography) than by what they are for (justice, mercy, truth-telling, forgiveness, love of enemies, and so much more). Who can blame people for being less than enthusiastic about such models of faith? This too is a form of grey.

So we've looked around, tested the water, searched for meaning. It's as if we've thrust ourselves into one new pursuit after another, convinced that this will finally be the means whereby lasting color can come into our world. But every time, the color fades, so that when we stop and look, all we can see is the colors of our pursuits melting into lifeless monochrome. Even religion doesn't satisfy.

ARTISANS OF HOPE

And then our eye catches something different. I've seen it in the eyes of a woman living in Pokhara, Nepal. Her smile is different. There's hope in her eyes. A refugee from Tibet, her parents led her across the Himalayas in the wake of the Red Guard Chinese revolution. In the process her feet were frostbitten, and she ended up in a Presbyterian hospital, where she heard about Jesus and became one of his followers. Since then, she's devoted her life to feeding, educating, and blessing Tibetan orphans. She's an artisan of hope, living her life in vibrant colors of joy and generosity, in spite of her relative poverty and her refugee status.

I've seen it in Nicanor, a tiny man from Nepal from whom joy oozes every time he speaks. His belief in Jesus' power to change lives, families, and villages is so great that he'd feel he was being selfish if he didn't share the good news of Jesus' invitation to a different life. Since the sharing of such news has, at various times, been illegal in Nepal, Nicanor's been in jail countless times. It's never bothered him, though, because in jail, just as much as outside, he's relentless in generously sharing the good news, encouraging his fellow prisoners by imparting hope and inviting them to a different life. Jailers grow tired of the effect he has on other prisoners, and so he's released. Off he goes to another village, where the whole thing starts all over again.

I've seen it in a friend in Africa named Walter, who's working hard to free women from sexual slavery. Once freed, they have needs for physical, emotional, and spiritual healing. Through his ministry they receive shelter, food, safety, and transformation, all in the name of Jesus.

There's Gahigi in Rwanda, who's mediating forgiveness between genocide perpetrators and victims day after day, even though he lost 142 family members to the killings.

Splashes of color are everywhere, even in the prosperous West. Dr. Paul is on the front lines anywhere on the planet there's been a crisis, imparting physical blessing in Jesus' name. Another person teaches gardening to inner-city children and teens, spilling the color green into the grey world of project housing and crime, shattered families and addictions. Another young man has parlayed his knitting skills (learned, hilariously, in high school as a means of raising cash for prom night) into an economic development enterprise for Ugandan women. He and his friends teach ladies to knit, then buy their ski hats and return to the States to sell them.

What do all these people have in common? They've responded to an invitation to paint with the colors of hope by stepping into the story God is writing across the canvas of history. People like this are scattered throughout the pages of time and across the continents of geography. Each of them has been, for me, a little bit like the girl in red. My eye has been drawn to them as the embodiment of hope, the possibility of beauty, the resurrection of meaning.

To know such hope is asking a lot, especially in these days of tremendous upheaval and global uncertainty. "Security" seems a quaint and antiquated notion, threatened as we are by terror and international catastrophes. We are also undermined by economic trauma, as the seeds of excess sown over past decades finally begin to germinate their poisonous flower. Foreclosures, layoffs, downsizing, and outsourcing have become such commonplace news themes that they don't shock us anymore—they only bring a sense of dread so that the only hope we have is the hope that it won't happen to us. If this is the extent of our hope, then the paradigm of our life becomes nothing more than disaster, which seems a far cry from the artistry of abundant living to which Jesus invites us.

The stunning reality of Jesus' invitation is that I'm called to more, much more, than simply surviving, protecting my assets and reputation while, as a footnote, I drop a little money in the offering and tell my neighbors Jesus died for them. Such a small view of God's activity in my life, and God's calling on my days, is part of the reason so many find Christianity boring. But let's not confuse this caricature of the Christian life with the real thing, the genuinely life-giving words of the Master. From the very beginning Jesus' vision of following him has entailed the notion of living outwardly. Trusting in God's active involvement in our daily lives, we're invited to learn dependence on the Creator for provision, direction, and protection. Then, from this place of security, we're invited to live outwardly, finding creative ways to spill hope into the world.

I ponder what it might be like to become someone who embodies this substantive hope, able to paint the vibrant colors of God's good reign onto this world's canvas. Millions of people through the ages have walked such a road, pursued such a life. Maybe the same could be true for us. If the Bible has anything to say about it, I'm sure it's true for you, because this is, in fact, the life for which we were created, and though we might settle for less, we'll never be truly satisfied with less.

THREE MOVEMENTS

Learning to live that kind of life is what this book is all about. Part 1 helps us capture the kind of picture God is painting in this beautiful yet broken world. Based on God's character, and the teachings of Jesus, we're invited to envision a much different place than the one we presently inhabit. It's this vision of hope that will become our north star as we use the life we've been given to spill forth God's hope.

Part 2 is about the colors that create hope, because it's not enough to see what kind of world God is creating; we must have the right paints on our palette if we're going to pull it off. Religion is complex, layered with rituals, obligations, fears, reputations to protect, and experts continually arguing about doctrinal nuances and ethical priorities and mandates. The good news is we can step away from that and find a clear path toward our calling as artists by learning the colors needed to bless the world. Thankfully, God has shown us that hope, in its million different forms, always springs from three primary colors: justice, mercy, and love.

Part 3 reminds us that our calling to be people of hope needn't wait to begin until our lives are free of problems and challenges. If we postpone our art until things settle down, our calling to impart hope will always be just a day or two away. No. Redemption, transforming the canvas of our reality, must start now, right in the midst of our messes. Learning to live out our hopeful faith amongst the realities of our fallen world is what this section is all about. The good news is we'll discover that the very things we thought were barriers to becoming artisans of hope are what God will use to shape our souls, giving a depth to the colors we'll pour into the world.

ARTISTS NEEDED

As I write this introduction, the church finds itself in the headlines once again, for all the wrong reasons. There are revelations about a cover-up of sexual abuse in the Catholic church, and there are Christian militia groups arming in some states. Right in the middle of all this, there's a big argument about the "emergent church" and whether it's composed of truth or falsehood, as if something as ill-defined as this movement could be contained in either a sweeping endorsement or condemnation.

People are looking at all this and saying, "Just as I suspected—the church is a waste of time," or worse, "the church is less relevant than I even suspected." I hear it in my city—Seattle—and though I don't agree, I understand how people come to such conclusions. They see the church painting ugliness, arrogance, and lust on the canvas of this world, and so they walk or run away.

There's only one way to address this: We need to be painting different pictures—of justice, mercy, love, hospitality, celebration, and hope. This book is about learning to be the kind of people who live with this vision, who develop our collective skills as artisans.

It is urgent work, because splashes of beauty are needed on our world's canvas, now more than ever.

PART ONE

VISION

*To know what you prefer, instead of humbly saying Amen
to what the world tells you you ought to prefer,
is to have kept your soul alive.*

–ROBERT LOUIS STEVENSON

*He creates each of us by Christ Jesus to join him in the work
he does, the good work he has gotten ready for us to do,
work we had better be doing.*[1]

–PAUL THE APOSTLE

Because I'm a pastor, I've a foot in two utterly different worlds. I'm exposed, daily, to what I call the "Christian Economic Machine." My inbox is stuffed with unsolicited invitations to conferences about how to grow my church and make it "sticky" (so that new people don't leave), how to shrink my church by dividing it into little churches, how to hire staff and fire them, expand budgets and cut them, run programs and learn why programs are from the devil. Magazines offer more of the same: endless tinkering with structure in the hope that adding coffee or taking it away, adding the word *emergent* or despising it, will make our church better.

My second world is among people who don't get those e-mails. My calling is to shepherd them and teach them, and the truth is they don't care about the issues in those e-mails at all. They're trying to figure out what difference knowing Jesus and following him is supposed to make in their daily living. They're dealing with boatloads of suffering and joys, fears and hopes. They're trying to hold their singleness faithfully, or their marriage. They're trying to figure out what to do with the rest of their lives, whether they're university students, nearing retirement, or somewhere in between. They're dealing with issues related to health and sexuality, money and employment. And a common thread that runs through all their questioning is "What does following Christ have to do with these things?"

As a pastor I'd be wise to clear 90 percent of my inbox from the first world, and absorb *all* the questions and conversations related to the second. The first world feels like endless discussions about window dressing, as if changing our mission statement or adding candles to worship will make a church healthy. I know too many pastors who've been perpetually frustrated by such tinkering to believe that it's the right track. The second world, however, the world of real people seeking to live faithfully, contributes to the shaping of my own faith in profound ways.

I've been listening to people ask questions and tell me stories about the relationship of their faith to their real lives for the past twenty-five years. These conversations and my own study of the Bible have reshaped my understanding of what it means to be Christ followers.

I began my faith journey thinking we were lawyers on a mission. We understood the legal status of humanity as condemned and could explain, with great precision, why Christ's deity, humanity, death, and resurrection could change our sentence, in spite of our guilt. While that legal element remains foundational and important, I've come to discover that our calling is less lawyer, more artist.

Each of us is endowed by our Creator, through the gift of Christ's life, with the capacity to impart great gifts of beauty to this world. "Blessed to be a blessing" is how God said it to Abraham, and since we're in his great big family, as followers of Christ, his calling is our calling. There are particular offerings of beauty ("good works," Paul calls them in his letter to the Ephesians) that we are invited to share with our world. We are, in other words, artists.

This way of seeing my calling, of seeing our calling, has made all the difference. Becoming a faith artist is an invitation to joy, creativity, and profound adventure.

Unfortunately the tide of faith culture pushes away from art, toward law. This first section addresses these issues of identity because, until I see myself as an artist, I'll never get on with the work of painting the colors of God's good reign on my world.

Let the adventure begin.

FAITH ART

Cure for the Common Consumer

When we drug ourselves to blot out our soul's call, we are being good Americans and exemplary consumers.[1]

    —Steven Pressfield

There is no shortage of good days. It is good lives that are hard to come by.

    —Annie Dillard

I was sixteen years old when my high school band went to Europe. All of us had worked hard to get there. We did fundraising, mostly by selling raffle tickets for a Pontiac Firebird that a local dealer had donated to the cause. I decided to try selling my required allotment of tickets to the richest people possible. We were the Highlanders, so after school I'd get into my kilt and walk around Fresno, California, looking for doctors, dentists, and lawyers. I'd walk into their offices looking like a freak, tell them the story of our planned trip, and sell tickets. Most of these rich professionals would buy ten or twenty at a time.

My plan was wildly successful. Tickets sold. Music was learned. One night shortly after school ended in June, we loaded our instruments into big buses and drove all night down to Los Angeles, where we boarded a flight to London. Though we didn't know it at the time, dozens of life-changing experiences awaited us, from sledding in the Alps to standing at the top of the Eiffel Tower at midnight. Whole worlds opened before us we didn't even know existed, as most of us had never been on a plane, never been outside California. It was quite an education.

A moment of truth, though, early on, sort of divided the group into two camps. Our first part of the tour was in England, and just trying to cross the street nearly killed me, as I kept looking the wrong way before stepping out. By the time we arrived in Scotland, I was bone tired, suspicious of the many unknowns, and ready to go home. After a day that included an afternoon concert, we boarded a bus and made our way to Dunblane, where we stayed at a remarkable old hotel, sitting on the crest of a hill.

"You've free time tonight," we were told, "and there's Scottish folk dancing on the main floor, starting at nine, if you're interested." After supper, I made my way back to my room, where I intended to get lost in a Friday-night round of Crazy Eights with my roommates. It was a little after ten when the three of us, astonishingly, got a clue. We looked at each other, and someone said, "This is pathetic. We're in Scotland. We worked hard to get here. None of our friends have been to Europe. People are dancing and singing downstairs, and we're hiding in our room, playing cards! What are we doing?"

"We hate dancing," another chimed in, stating the obvious. The reality, though, wasn't that I hated dancing; it's just that I'd never danced, except for that one very painful time at middle-school homecoming when I summoned the courage of ten thousand warriors, approached Suzanne, and asked her to dance. Suzanne smiled that perfect, confident smile that makes eighth-grade boys feel like less evolved forms of life. "Yes," she said, holding out her hand as we made our way to the dance floor. Just touching her skin nearly made me faint. She danced like a goddess, which only contributed to my feelings of vast inferiority, leading me to believe I was her one "charity dance" for the evening. I swore then, I'd never dance again.

Nevertheless, when one brave soul stood up and said, "I'm going dancing anyway," I followed, leaving the other room-mate alone to play solitaire. "It will be fun to watch," I said to myself as we entered the large ballroom of the eighteenth-century castle, turned hotel. I'd settled the matter in my mind by convincing myself that guys always do the asking, and the simple way to save face would be to remain on the sidelines. My call. No problem. The room was full of townsfolk, as this was a real Scottish gathering, a monthly event. Everyone was dancing, laughing, shouting, and swinging each other around while we stood and watched.

Then it happened. A lovely lass, surely older but not by much, came over and, scarcely even asking, took my hand and led me onto the floor. I began to protest, but she just smiled and said, "It's fine, lad. Ye'll learn it soon enough!" With my heart in my throat, I listened as the teacher gave instructions, and then the fun began.

That's all it took. I stayed on the floor until the last dance at three A.M. The night ended with a bagpiper playing "Scotland the Brave" as the townsfolk held hands and sang, hugged, and wept. My dance partner thanked me, kissed me on the cheek, and walked into the night. I've loved the bagpipes and Scotland ever since. Of course, I could have played Crazy Eights instead and gone to sleep at eleven. The tragedy with such a course of action is that I would never have known what I missed.

FAITH DANCING OR CHURCH SITTING?

Every Sunday, in churches across the land, something profound will happen just before the preacher ascends to the pulpit to talk: the children will leave the building. They'll go somewhere else to be cared for by others, because, as God and all the rest of us know, children aren't wired to sit and listen to somebody talk for twenty, thirty, or forty minutes.

There are, of course, theories about developmental stages and children's limited capacity for thinking conceptually. They're not likely to be interested in the talk I'm going to give this weekend about imputed righteousness and the value of propitiation. In fact, if they were in the room and I started chatting about such stuff, I'd know immediately I was boring them; it would show in their active little bodies and wandering little eyes. They're not made for this.

They're made for dancing.

At the risk of losing my job (after all, I'm the guy who talks for forty minutes each Sunday), I'm going out on a limb to suggest we're not made for this either, at least not without some serious conditions and qualifications. The children are on to something. Yes, we adults have the developmental capacities for dealing with abstract ideas, and in this sense what I do each Sunday has value. But here's the problem: If we're only *hearing*, and not *doing*, we're playing Crazy Eights. Not only that, we are party to the massive deception that is spiritual consumerism.[2] It's numbing souls, weakening our churches, and so dimming the glorious light of Christ—the light God intends to shine through his people—that the darkness in the land is palpable.

If we'd been more like children, this wouldn't have happened. Children won't just sit; they must do something. Watch them sometime, intently, so you can learn how to play. We were with friends in Germany this past winter. Their three-year-old son and I were able to bridge the language barrier by playing catch. I'd toss him a ball and he'd try to catch it, sometimes even succeeding. The grin wouldn't leave his face. You could offer him any sort of passive activity instead: television, reading a book, discussing theology, and he'd prefer the doing. The same thing happens when small children have Play-Doh or paint. They'll do, and do, and do some more. *Creating* is what they live for.

Consuming is what they're taught. Over time we learn it's easier, and less risky to one's esteem, to watch passively than jump in, to sit on the sidelines rather than dance. As we grow older, we refine the skill of consumption until it becomes us. We watch TV instead of lingering in conversation over meals. We collect paintings rather than make them. We watch sports rather than play them. We eat out rather than try new recipes and create incredible (or sometimes, less so) meals.

Of course, I'm generalizing. All of us have moments and areas where we shine. But it's important to see this trajectory from childhood to adulthood: we seem to move inexorably toward habits of consumption that wound, sometimes fatally, our creative self.

Too often, our God-given creative capacities and calling are buried beneath layers of obligations and cultural expectations. Many are missing out on finding the joy and energy that comes from creating because we've been schooled in consumerism more than creativity. We've learned what we can't do; learned that the professionals will always outclass us so it's better not to try; learned that it's easier to consume than create; learned to avoid the risk of failure. As a result, we're sitting in the concert hall rather than standing on stage; or we're in the bleachers rather than on the field.

Everything that will unfold in these pages is based on the premise that there's artistry and beauty in all of us waiting to find expression, like seeds waiting to germinate. Each of us is made by God with specific creative capacities, as the great apostle spelled out in his letter to the Ephesians.[3] We're invited to use these capacities to bless, painting the colors *hope* and *beauty* onto the canvas of our broken world, each of us in unique ways. When this happens, hospitals are built, wells are dug, women are freed from sexual slavery, warring tribes reconcile and forgive, neighbors are loved and served, parties are thrown, forests are restored, art is created, children are taught, schools are built, the elderly are dignified, cars are repaired. You get the picture.

A MATTER OF LIFE AND DEATH

My wife and I ran a Bible school in the wilderness for many years. When guests would come to us, one of our favorite things to do was guide them up a mountain and throw them off— attached to a rope, of course. We call that rappelling, and our guests loved it. We found, though, we often needed to give the knot-tying lecture more than once. We'd give it the first time, talking about how to examine the rope for fraying, demonstrating its strength, explaining how to wear, tighten, and check the harness, and showing how to tie the right knots. Then we'd go outside to a climbing wall on the side of our house, and they'd watch as we showed them how to descend and how to protect someone who was descending by belaying them.

They'd listen politely, but in truth most of them were either bored or eager to do what they'd come there to do—get up on the mountains and have adventures. Our last word was: "Now that we've shown all this, you'll be able to tie knots for each other, and check each other's harnesses for safety. Oh, and you'll be doing the belaying too."

That's when everything would stop, and the color would

drain from everyone's faces. Sheepishly, but invariably, they'd ask, "Can you run through that once more?" Happy to accommodate, we'd explain everything a second time, fully aware that in reality this was the first time most of them were paying attention, because this time the stuff we were talking about had immediate, first-person relevance to their situation. People listened like their life depended on it, because it did!

Jesus did the spiritual equivalent of this all the time; for instance, when he sent his followers out and told them to do things like heal the sick and cleanse lepers.[4] It was the doing that gave relevance to the hearing, and the hearing that energized them for the doing. We seem to have misplaced this marvelous synergy. Too often the church has fallen into the trap of equating knowledge with maturity. We've elevated sitting, listening, and absorbing content—with the goal of improving our personal condition—to the pinnacle of maturity. We reward children when they memorize chunks of the Bible.

Now, I'm a big fan of encountering God through reading, studying, and memorizing the Bible. Jesus knew the Bible well; however, he also knew the dangerous possibilities of its misuse.[5] If those big chunks that are flooding little heads don't find application in real activities, the only motivation they have for getting Bible knowledge is the sticker they'll win. As soon as they graduate and the stickers stop coming, we'll have taught them that knowing the Bible is good for awards and nothing more. Some of them will become part of the large statistical crowd between ages eighteen and thirty that's leaving the church.

I don't blame them for leaving. After all, they've been taught that following Jesus means sitting and listening to someone talk. It means poring over the minutia of a book as if it's a legal code to be memorized and debated. They've learned that the big issues of the church have to do with whether this brand of Christianity is "more right" than that brand, and whether "emergent" is better than "neo-Calvinist," as if these labels are somehow important. Thus it is that Jesus' followers fight each other over minutiae while sometimes ignoring clearly pressing matters.[6] Meanwhile, all they're taught about the grey and tattered canvas of this world is that it's going to get worse before it gets better, and burned up in the end, so don't waste your time painting. They've been taught, in other words, that following Jesus has little to do with their longings for meaning and making a difference. As consumers, they move on in search of a better product.

SPIRITUAL CONSUMERISM GETS UGLY

I remember meeting someone whose mother attended a church that met for Bible study six nights a week. People would bring big notebooks and learn about the original Greek and Hebrew meaning of every word. The teacher went through the whole thing, literally verse by verse, for years. My friend's mom amassed closets full of notes along with cassette tapes of every sermon. She could tell you the meaning of every Hebrew phrase in Isaiah 53, could explain how Jesus would return, and make some educated guesses regarding when. She knew her Bible better than anyone I'd met.

And she hated her daughter. *Hated* her. She'd write scathing letters, sickly weaving together tender hints of affection with violent threats should her daughter continue in her "wicked ways," which meant nothing more than living a life of her own choosing. Apparently all that Bible teaching and information didn't lead to any sort of decency or charity on the part of the mom. To the contrary, it became ammunition for manipulation. The Bible became a weapon, and in the hands of someone who attends church six nights a week, learning every linguistic nuance of the text, it can be a wicked weapon indeed.

My friend's mom didn't invent the misuse of Scripture and religion. The Crusades and the Inquisition were murder, torture, and theft in Jesus' name. Colonialism? One African pastor said, "You told us to close our eyes and pray to receive Jesus, and when we opened them, you'd stolen our land." People have quoted directly from the Bible to justify slavery, genocide, and abusive patriarchy, all in Jesus' name.

When people of faith begin believing their highest calling is to sit and listen to their teachers, they'll become prey to all sorts of destructive ideas, as history has so amply displayed. Passive religionists will flow like water along the path of least resistance, and if this means they're called to hate Jews, they'll hate Jews while continuing to sit in church and sing hymns. If it means they're called to treat Africans as subhuman and steal their land, they'll treat Africans as subhuman and steal their land. If they're called to worship free markets, or socialist markets, they'll worship free markets or socialist markets. Consumers are passive and open to manipulation.[7] This is most assuredly not what Jesus had in mind for us.

Those who see themselves as artists, however, aren't so easily swayed. They've spent long hours looking at Jesus' vision for the canvas that is this world. They've come to understand the beauty of justice, the glory of intimacy, the joy of service and hospitality, the profound life-giving character of generosity, and the stunning colors of grace. They know what belongs on the canvas. When a teacher comes along advocating anti-Semitism, they won't blindly follow, they'll resist.[8] Their commitment isn't to attending religious shows, it's to painting the colors of hope onto the canvas of our world. They're artists, and they know it.

THE LORD OF THE DANCE

The moments of truth come in our lives when Jesus invites us to dance. He walks up to us and holds out his hand, tells us there's dancing work to be done. It's joyous, creative, life-giving work. We're intimidated by the boatloads of our own failure, by the chains of consumerism that have kept us shackled to the recliner in front of the TV. His hand is there waiting. We recoil, but like the Scottish lass, he says, "It's fine. Ye'll learn soon enough," and we need to decide. Will we become artists or remain consumers?

Moses is chilling in the desert and God invites him to become an artist instead. He does this same thing with Jeremiah, and Hannah, and Mary, and Paul. And you. His hand is outstretched, as he invites you to the dance of creativity and beauty, and you need to choose: artist, or consumer?

When Jesus was wrapping up his days on earth, he didn't tell us to go to church. He didn't tell us to engage in a spiritualized version of channel surfing, as we hop from place to place in search of just the right programming to entertain us. He told us to get out and actually do the stuff he'd already been doing, painting the hope of God's reign on the canvas of God's world. He told us we're *artists*.

The learning begins by following Jesus into the real world, leaving consumerism behind, and learning to see what's actually there on the canvas that is our glorious and broken world.

2

CANVAS

The Art of Waking Up

One climbs, one sees. One descends, one sees no longer. But one has seen. There is an art of conducting oneself in the lower regions by the memory of what one saw higher up.

    —René Daumal

If you want to be somebody, if you want to go somewhere, you'd better wake up and pay attention.

    —Sister Mary Clarence, in Sister Act 2

Do you see this woman?

    —Jesus

I was the visiting teacher at a Bible school a few years ago and was speaking from the Old Testament story about Jacob and his brother, Esau. "The two of them couldn't have been more different," I said, after which I went on to describe Jacob as the one who liked to stay home and cook, tugging on his mom's apron and keeping his hands clean. In the Bible he's called a "smooth man."[1] I began poking fun at Jacob by reading the narrative and making his voice sound stereotypically gay, in stark contrast to Esau, whose voice I made to sound like a football player who failed high school English.

The ploy was good for a few laughs, but at the end of the session a student came up to me, obviously holding back some anger, with tears in his eyes. "I hope you'll never do that again when you teach Genesis in the future," he said. I couldn't imagine what I'd done to offend him. I asked and he stalled, hesitating to give me an answer until everyone had left the room. Then he said, "I'm struggling with my sexuality, okay. And when you talk that way, you're just making it that much easier for people to stereotype us, to continue hating and mistreating us."

His words stung, but I knew he was right about what I'd done. I apologized and asked him to share more. For the next little while I listened as his layers of defensiveness came down and he poured out his heart. With tears he offered more of his story, including alienation from his Christian parents once he told them he was dealing with same-sex attraction; they rejected him before he even began acting on these sexual temptations. When he shared the issue with the leaders of his church, they told him he was not allowed to attend. These rejections left him with nowhere to go, and the isolation led, eventually, to promiscuity and all the loneliness, shame, guilt, and life-shrinking fallout that comes with it. By the time he shared these parts of his story, I was pierced with his pain and crying too.

Finally he talked about the role Jesus had played in helping him move from promiscuity to celibacy, supported by close Christian friends of both genders who knew him well, loved him, and supported him. He told me he didn't know where following Jesus would ultimately take him, but that he was there at Bible school because Jesus had offered him more hope than anything or anyone else out there. Silence filled the room as the weight of his words began sinking in. I wondered how many people were sitting in churches singing praise songs about how strong they are in Christ, terrified to unveil their struggles for fear of the very kind of rejection he'd experienced.

He continued. "But here's what's sad: Many times, when I really begin to think I'm turning a corner, I hear someone put a label on people like me again, like you did today, and it sends me into a spiral of depression that ranges from anger to self-loathing. You need to learn how to see us as people."

As I returned to my room that night, I knew this conversation would remain in my memory. One particular phrase from his last words sunk deep into my heart: *"You need to learn how to see."*

This student was right. He blew apart my categories. In the past, if you'd asked, "Do you see this man?" I would have said, "Of course." But the truth would have been that much of what I presumed to know about this particular person was wrong. I had eyes. I perceived. *But I did not see.*

The church has a wide reputation for not seeing. As I write this, countless aid groups are digging through the rubble of a massive earthquake in Haiti, the poorest nation in the Western Hemisphere. As is always the case when there's a flood, earthquake, or fire, some prominent TV evangelist has declared it to be the judgment of God. The same thing happened on 9/11 and when New Orleans flooded. "God is mad because of sin, and the earthquake is his vengeance." You begin to understand a popular bumper sticker: "Lord, deliver me—from your followers." We have the capacity to be an exceptionally ugly and judgmental lot, in Jesus' name.

We will never become the people of hope and blessing we're

meant to be until we learn how to wake up and pay attention to the glory and pain, beauty and suffering that are in lives all around us. This waking up is what artists call "seeing," and without it, our religion gets very ugly, because we become experts, not at loving people, but at putting people in categories and judging them, which is a sport that's been around for as long as there's been religion.

SIMON SEES?

"Do you see this woman?" Jesus asks Simon the Pharisee.[2] What a silly question, Jesus. Of course Simon sees this woman. In fact, from Simon's perspective, it was you, Jesus, who didn't "see this woman." When she burst into the party, uninvited, and began weeping at your feet, wiping the tears with her hair, and anointing you with expensive perfume, Simon saw her with perfect clarity. He even had a label for her: *whore*.

Simon not only saw the woman, he saw Jesus clearly too, now that this unpleasant scene had unfolded. All his doubts about Jesus' dubious claims to be Messiah were now confirmed. *If this man were a prophet, he would know that this woman is a sinner.*[3] Simon probably felt pretty good about the evening. One quick glance at the whore kissing the feet of the alleged Messiah, and both parties can be dismissed, the former as a sinner and the latter as a blasphemer.

It would fit so perfectly, were it not for the untidy fact that Simon doesn't really see anything with any clarity or accuracy. He doesn't see that this woman is prostrate before Jesus as a genuine worshiper, doesn't see that her encounter with him has changed her forever. He doesn't even see the *possibility* of her transformation, let alone the reality of it. He doesn't see her love, doesn't see her lavish expressions of uninhibited worship. All he sees is a prostitute. And because he misreads her by slapping a label on her rather than really looking, he does the same thing to Jesus. That Jesus would allow her to touch him proves he's not all-knowing, and if he's not all-knowing, he's not a prophet. Case closed.

THE LABELS WE USE

From our earliest days, we're taught to label everything so that we can communicate. This is all well and good for infants and foreign language students, but not at all appropriate for grown-ups learning about our beautiful and broken world.

Look at that woman, walking downtown on Second Avenue. Her clothes are dirty, her hair unkempt. She's wearing a small torn backpack and carrying a black plastic garbage bag. Did I mention that her shoes have holes? And that she's walking slowly, as if she has nowhere to go?

"Homeless," you say to yourself, and you're right. There. You've slapped a label on her. The label, though, doesn't just sit there. When you slap a label on someone, you're usually backing up a big dump truck of assumptions and pouring them all over that person. *Homeless* means lazy and uneducated, probably promiscuous too. She's no doubt made a host of stupid decisions in her life that have gotten her into this mess. Oh, and don't get too close; she's likely carrying an infectious disease.

The problem is that you've stolen her personhood and made her an object. The reasons for homelessness run the spectrum: mental illness, domestic violence, bad financial choices, working poor who can't afford shelter, illness and lack of adequate health insurance, laziness, choice. You can't know *her* reasons without taking the time to know *her*.

The point Jesus was trying to make with Simon is that learning to see is an art.

WAKING UP TO THE ART OF SEEING

Juliette is among the great contemporary artists in America. She travels all over the country giving seminars that teach people how to paint in the classical atelier style, which means that those who study with her learn to paint what's actually there rather than their subjective interpretation of what's there. As a result, her students' works look more like Rembrandt than Duchamp, or even Van Gogh. We've displayed their works with great pride in our church building in Seattle.

Of course, learning to paint this way requires tremendous discipline, especially the discipline of "seeing." In hopes of learning more about what it means to see clearly, I called and asked her if I could visit one of her classes and talk about the relationship of faith and art, which is how I ended up in her art school on a cold November morning.

I enter the old brick building and make my way down a long hallway toward the door that marks her classroom. I enter silently and watch her students in action. In a warm, bright room, about a dozen students are scattered in a semicircle, all painting the same subject, a beautiful woman sitting on a stool. Each is intent on capturing the essence of the subject on his/her canvas. Juliette whispers to me as we walk past each student's work, explaining that the semicircle is a sort of one-room schoolhouse, which is why some students are drawing, others are using charcoal, and others are beginning to paint, as they learn to address the nuances of light and shadow.

One of the students is asking Juliette a question about the disconnect between what he's seeing and wanting to create and what's actually appearing on his canvas. He's clearly frustrated by the process. Juliette answers, in essence, "You're just beginning to see. Keep showing up and you will see with greater clarity, and that will change everything."

We won't get very far at all unless we *want* to see. These students are taking four years out of their lives, investing their hard-earned money, and subjecting themselves to tremendous discipline because they want to both see and create beauty.

Wanting to see is critical here. Matthew recalls the story of two blind men sitting by the side of the road.[4] When they heard Jesus would be passing by, they began shouting, "Lord, Son of David, have mercy on us!" What do they want? They want their eyes opened, they want to perceive the world that's really there, as fully as possible. They want to see!

Without *wanting* to see we won't, so maybe we should begin by considering whether or not we want to enlarge our perception capacities. At first glance, the thought of even asking seems silly. Of course I do. But on further reflection, I realize it's an entirely legitimate and important question, because the testimony of the Bible is that humanity is prone over and over to choose darkness over light, blindness instead of sight, foolishness over wisdom. And why not?

The challenge is that seeing will change me in unforeseen ways, and I might not like that. Until I see homeless people through the eyes of Jesus, I'm free to put them in a box and leave them alone. All that changes when God opens my eyes. Suddenly I'm called to compassion (which means "to suffer with"), generosity, solidarity. This is disruptive. Life is full enough already, with our own plans and agendas. It's far easier to keep labeling than actually seeing.

Having a desire to see clearly implies that I don't see clearly already. This is where I believe a lot of Christians struggle. We begin a relationship with Jesus, and then as we sit in Bible studies over the years, our understanding of who God is, who we are, and where history is heading begins to calcify. Without even realizing it, we soon have a grid in place that enables us to objectify everything: people, political parties, churches.

WHAT'S IN YOUR HERESY BIN?

When I was in seminary, a missionary was teaching our missions class and telling us a story about casting demons out of a man while visiting a tribe in Africa. When he mentioned the name Jesus as he spoke, the man, chained to a tree, started foaming at the mouth and broke the chains, charging at the missionary and trying to kill him. Our instructor explained how he prayed and literally cast a demon out of the man.

In my seminary we didn't hear many amazing stories like this, so I was completely captivated, along with most of the class. One student, however, sat in the back, his feet on the desk, his arms folded, his countenance utterly unreceptive, even defiant. When the teacher asked if he had any questions, his response stunned me: "No questions. Just a comment. Casting demons out of people ended when the Bible was fully written, about 300 AD." With one easy assessment this young student freed himself from having to reconsider his view and from ever having to worry about encountering someone possessed with demons. Somewhere along the way he'd picked up the notion that all miracles had ceased, and so when he heard someone talking about a miracle, he immediately tossed that person's experience, if not that entire person, into his heresy bin.

Some people have heresy bins the size of Texas. I remember reading about one pastor who, at the end of his life, would only take communion with himself, so convinced was he that he alone saw truth. Another group knew their Scriptures so well they put Jesus to death on a cross, perfectly convinced because of all their training that he wasn't the Messiah.[5] Let's not forget the Catholics inquisitioning the Protestants and the Lutherans persecuting the radical reformers. Everyone had it right; except they didn't. For most who'd settled into these camps, they were finished seeing anything new. They'd live out their days defending their opinion, even if it was wrong.

Only those who remain teachable and moldable all their days will continue to see with increasing clarity. I think of my friend Major Ian Thomas, who was ninety-three when he died. He'd been preaching since he was eighteen. His Bible had seen countless covers and was thick from use and markings. I was with him one Sunday morning a few months before his death, and what struck me most in our moments together was that when he turned on the television to watch a favorite pastor of his, he asked me to bring him his Bible. I did, and watched as he opened it and carefully followed along.

After seventy-five years of teaching in dozens of countries, my friend was still eager to receive and learn. On the other hand, I've met people who've been Christians five years who come across like they already have everything figured out because they've bought into some system. The system becomes their grid. Their grid becomes their means of objectifying; in the process, the thing that's lost is their capacity to see.

THE ART OF PAYING ATTENTION

Back at the art school, Juliette and I leave the classroom and move to a different studio, where numerous objects are scattered on shelves and in corners, with bright lights shining on them. "This is where we begin," she says to me, pointing to a plain white sphere about the size of a softball. A reading lamp is pointed directly at it, flooding it with ample light and, of course, shadow.

"Their first assignment is to draw this ball, in the setting of this light. I tell the students they'll need at least twenty hours to paint this. Of course, they don't believe me. But at the end of twenty hours, there are always some students who come to me and say, 'Can I have more time? I'm just starting to *really see* what's there.'" Juliette smiles and says, "That's really the point, isn't it? Before we can become artists, *all of us need to learn how to truly see.*" She points to a thin sliver on the ball where light moves to shadow, not instantly, but in a gloriously seamless transition. "This is what they need to see if they'll ever be able to paint," she says, her eyes smiling as she advocates for the need we all have to become children again so that our world creates enough wonder in us that we start paying attention.

Suddenly, there in the studio, I find myself beginning to look at all the objects around me in an entirely different light (pun intended). Take that coffee mug over there, sitting by the window. In my previous life, before I became an artist (twenty minutes ago), I would have quickly assessed the shape and given it a label: cup. But now that I'm really looking, I'm seeing more. The reflections of light caught by the ceramic finish, the brilliant transition from light to shadow, and the way that transition is exploited by shapely lines have conspired to transform my vision. I'm not looking at a container for my coffee anymore; I'm looking at a work of art.

PAYING ATTENTION TO OUR WORLD

Paul pays attention to culture when, in Acts, we find him observing "the city full of idols."[6] Many Christians wouldn't bother looking. "All people need is Jesus, and all I need to share Jesus is a Bible," they say, standing on a street corner, shouting answers to questions nobody is asking. They don't know how to paint the gospel on the canvas of their culture because they don't know their culture.

In contrast, Luke's language indicates Paul is *carefully observing* the idols of the culture. What's more, this man raised in Judaism knows enough about the Greek poets to quote their poetry as a means of sharing the gospel with the Greek citizens of Athens. Every culture, including ours, has idols and poets, and we'd do well to spend time "carefully observing" them, because within them we'll find both the questions and answers that are already lines on the canvas of our world, waiting, as it were, for someone to come and fill in the colors.

Some friends came over and we watched *Blood Diamond* together a few years ago. A major theme of the movie is the kidnapping of a son into forced slavery, and his father's relentless pursuit of him. As fear and hate become ingrained in the son, the father risks everything to find and free the son, and then the son rejects him. Still, the father pursues. "We're seeing the gospel right now," one of our friends said, and she was right. I recently used the scenes of this man's relentless love for his son to show our church a marvelous picture of a father's heart. "We're the ones whose hearts have been stolen," I said, "and God is the Father pursuing us, relentlessly." The story is our own poets' portrayal of the gospel, explaining Jesus' parable about the shepherd seeking the lost sheep.

We'll only be able to share what the poets have to offer if we close our Bibles once in a while and read the *New York Times*, go to a concert, or watch a movie. I've found this commitment to "seeing" my world to be liberating and heartbreaking, as I've been pierced by the beauty, longing, darkness, glory, and pathos that had been there all along, but just outside my line of vision because I'd been taught it was unspiritual to look.

PAYING ATTENTION TO OURSELVES

Years ago I went to a marriage seminar at our church. Of course, it's not that I needed the seminar because, you see, I'm the senior pastor, and we leadership types, we're examples. No, I only went to set the example so that others would go. Sure enough, lots of couples did go, and I secretly patted myself on the back as I noted, among the attendees, those whose marriages I'd already assessed as train wrecks waiting to happen.

Nothing in my wildest imagining could have prepared me for what happened that day. The speaker's style wasn't engaging to me, but I was dutifully listening, even taking a few notes, again for the purpose of "setting an example." At the end of the morning, he gave us couples an assignment. We were to go somewhere far enough away that our quiet conversations couldn't be heard. Then, in the privacy of our own space, we were to share a time when as children we were hurt by something that was taken from us.

Everyone around is whispering, and while my wife is talking I hear muted laughter coming from the couple next to us as they share an intimate moment. When it's my turn to share, I begin to speak about a memory of coming home from a long trip with my high school band, the same trip I talked about in the previous chapter. I'd been in Europe nearly a month, and our bus was pulling into the parking lot of the school. Parents were there with cameras, signs, siblings. They were waving, shouting. I'm telling my wife this, and then I stop. And I start crying. I'm embarrassed, but when I try to stop, instead of gaining control, a floodgate of grief opens and I burst forth loud, heaving sobs, so that everyone in the room is staring at me. I go outside with my wife and continue weeping until I gain enough self-control to tell her that all my friends loaded into cars and went home. The bus drove away, and there I stood, alone, in the searing heat and isolation of that summer afternoon. I was gone for a month, and being left alone after my friends were gone was incredibly painful.

Revisiting that pain was a turning point in our marriage, for my wife and I both began to see how this kind of rejection, which I'd worked so hard to hide, was bubbling up. I'd become a very demanding husband, insisting that my wife "be there" for me, beyond all reasonable limits of what healthy love really is. But the change began with a painful seeing that I'd been working hard to ignore.

There are hidden places deep in each of our hearts, and our own growth and transformation are contingent on whether we're willing to look at what's there. God orchestrated some circumstances where I had the space to really see myself, and it's made all the difference. We need to give God space to show us who we really are, to show us our wounds, our gifts, our passions, our fears, our hidden addictions.

This is what Jesus meant when he told us that if we remain in him, we will know the truth, and the truth will set us free. Yes, we'll be liberated, yet not before facing ourselves and holding up our pain to the light of Jesus' healing and transforming powers.

Letting the scales drop from our eyes so that we begin to see what's really there, in our hearts and in our world, is the starting point. As long as we persist in jumping to sound bytes, clichés, and stereotypes instead of allowing our senses to be overwhelmed with the beauty and suffering that's all around us, we'll continue to be blind. Our inability to see will shrink our world, and our creative capacities to be a blessing will never be released. Those who let themselves move into the terrifying spaces of heartbreaking beauty and tragedy, of pain and glory, will see. They'll mourn and rejoice, laugh and weep. Their seeing will make moving into God's story inevitable, and they'll bless the world.

SUBJECT MATTERS
The Art of God's Reign

Should we not start with the most obvious fact of existence, that whoever is responsible is a fierce and incomparable artist beside whom all human achievement and creativity dwindle as child's play?[1]

–Philip Yancey

I like your Christ. I do not like your Christians. Your Christians are so unlike your Christ.

—Mahatma Gandhi

Juliette, my artist friend, knows her family tree down to its trunk, all the way back to the thirteenth century. She's Jewish, and to read her tree is to read the story of anti-Semitism, often carried out in the name of Christ. Her grandfather, whose family name was Bendheim, lived in the small German village of Bensheim, and he is purported to have been the only family member from there to survive the holocaust. His story is a remarkable testimony to the power of courage and resilience in the midst of paralyzing fear and darkness.

The stories of persecution and survival that constitute Juliette's heritage became seeds planted deep in her heart soil, where they would remain hidden, even to her at some level, until an event commenced germination. That event happened recently when a Jewish community center in London, Ontario, publicized an art contest, asking for submissions under the theme "Holocaust Survivors." The winning submission would eventually be a part of their collection.

Juliette says, "I knew the painting I needed to make as soon as I read about the contest. I could see it in my mind and within an hour I'd sketched out the big themes of the work." The painting, *Bendheim Remembrance,* is stunning, capturing the agony of the holocaust in ways beyond what words or overt violence ever could convey. It sits in her studio, and those who take the time to sit with the piece and pay attention to it will be changed by the looking. It is profound, filled with pathos—art for the ages.

I was looking at it one day and was particularly struck by the face of the man leaving Bendheim. Juliette looks at me, looking at him, and says, "He was hard to find. I hired the female model early on, but the right man for the picture eluded me. Then one day I saw him, eating in a Vietnamese restaurant on Capitol Hill. It was embarrassing, but I walked up to him, right in the midst of his meal, told him about the work I was doing, and asked him if he'd pose for it."

He agreed, and that's how an Ashkenazi Jewish pediatrician in Seattle became a model for a powerful work of art, created for a contest in Toronto about the slaughter of Jews in Germany. For linear thinkers, this kind of thing gets a little bizarre, but the reality is that Juliette saw him and knew immediately this was the man who was supposed to be in the painting. She'd been waiting for him before she met him because she knew the face she was looking for. Armed with that vision, she waited, watching, looking, living. When she finally saw her subject, she knew.

A GOOD SUBJECT IS HARD TO FIND

People often come to Christ the same way. They see the gospel, see Christ made visible, and say, though not usually in these words, "This is what I've been waiting for and didn't even know it."

When our church ran a medical clinic for a Nepali village, Hindus came to receive treatment because they had nowhere else to take their sick children, or their decaying teeth, or their ulcerated stomachs. Our team of Americans and Nepalese treated everyone equally, with charity and professionalism. At the end of our time there, the local church slaughtered some animals, offering a big feast to thank us for serving them and to share with us the impact our work was already having on their community.

Sitting around the fire at our outdoor feast, the Nepalese pastor shared stories of how threatened the Hindus had been in recent years by the presence of a church in the village, with the result that Christians had been persecuted for their faith. Our host had been in jail for preaching, and the church building had been burned and vandalized several times. People who'd come to Christ had their businesses blackmailed. In spite of all these hardships, the Christ followers living in the village were committed to loving their neighbors, even if their neighbors happened to be their enemies.

Our clinic treated more Hindus than Christians during our three-day stay. At the final feast the pastor told us he'd heard many stories from Hindus who'd been to the clinic and received help. Some of them said they'd be joining their celebrations on Sunday and considering Christ because they'd never seen any love like this before. Who loves those who torment and persecute them? Jesus' people, that's who.

Theologians debate what is meant by the Preacher's cryptic declaration in Ecclesiastes about God putting "eternity in the hearts of men."[2] However it's interpreted, one thing we cannot deny: It is part of the human condition for us to have some very good longings rattling around in our souls. Most of the time we delight in seeing justice, mercy, rest, abundance. We like good food with friends and recoil when earthquakes kill thousands or children are abused. These good longings are in us, sometimes buried and distorted, but there nonetheless.

As a result, seeing charity and kindness, creations of beauty, or moments of intimacy can have a profound effect on our souls, which is precisely what happened in Nepal. It's as if, to contradict Bono, we've finally "found what we're looking for." We see Mother Teresa caring for the poorest of the poor, or John Perkins working for justice in Mississippi, or Paul Brand working with lepers in India when he could be making lots of money in North America, and something in us says, "Yes! This is the way it's supposed to be. This is the kind of world I want to live in." Like Juliette, we've found our subject, the art we're called to put on the canvas, and its name is *hope*, the hope that is found in the reign of Christ.

This, of course, is the very thing Jesus did, every day of his life. He healed the sick, cared for the poor and marginalized, and taught his followers to do the same thing so God's good reign might become visible. Of course, not everyone was thrilled with his methods and ethics, and that is a story in itself. But for many, his way of living resonated with something inside, and they left everything and followed him. When we find the subject for our painting, we just know it.

FINDING THE SUBJECT NAMED *HOPE*

After I finished seminary, a strange set of circumstances (more details later) that can best be described as the movement of God landed me on a remote island, serviced only by ferries, in the northwest corner of the northwest corner of the United States. My wife and I had moved there from Los Angeles, and our new location was nearly the opposite of our previous home in every way. We'd moved from sun to clouds, urban to rural, dry to wet, huge to tiny, brown to green.

But perhaps the greatest shift of all was the contrast in spirituality between the big city and the island. Los Angeles was the entertainment capital of the world, awash in cash, fame, and upward mobility. The island could barely receive TV stations and was populated by spiritual seekers of every stripe. This was the land of organic gardens and homemade futons, spiritual crystals and New Age enlightenment, Buddhist retreat centers and movements to save the whales. These were people with master's degrees in philosophy driving beater pickups and making minimum wage so that they could live in a place of peace, where you could spend your evenings sitting on the beach by a fire, with a bottle of wine, watching whales breach as the sun set. How far from LA can you get?

I was now the pastor of a tiny congregation, and every week I'd open the Bible and preach. We'd sing, pray, often eat some food together. We surely enjoyed one another, enjoyed studying and learning what God had to say about life, death, morality, and the life everlasting, amen. We were, by many measures, a healthy congregation.

In spite of this, though, I felt a gigantic chasm between our life as a church and what the rest of our islanders were seeking and how they were living. These were the days when evangelicals were practicing a kind of baptized McCarthyism. Popular Christian books and speakers were intent on warning us about the cults of our world disguised as angels of light. "These people" worshiped nature rather than exercising dominion over it, we were told. "These people" questioned the unlimited economic growth needed to keep the wheels of capitalism running, so they were, according to these Bible teachers, obviously socialists, advocating laziness and land theft. "These people" were seducing naïve Christians into thinking that peace was a possibility in spite of Jesus' warnings about "wars and rumors of wars." "These people" were vegetarians, democrats, and, though they didn't necessarily know it, agents of Satan himself.

What I came to discover through coaching Little League, refereeing basketball, and playing music with locals was that the "these people" popular evangelical authors were warning me about were my neighbors. The church office was in a building that also housed the workspace of an organic gardener/artist and a philosophy major/graphic designer. Both, through their lifestyles and their ideas, could have walked off the pages of these anti–New Age books I was reading.

It wouldn't be wise, in my opinion, to share the good news of Christ by walking up and telling these people they're children of

Satan. Heaven and hell and who's going where weren't subjects on the tips of their tongues either, so that also didn't seem like the right starting point. Though I didn't know it at the time, I was looking for the right subject for my painting. "What will help these people see the hope found in Christ?" was the question behind my searching back then, and it's still my question today.

Looking for a good role model for how to interact with people who didn't know Christ, I decided to read about Jesus' encounters with people and, from that, determine how to proceed. Try it sometime. Just sit there and read through the Gospels, looking for major themes Jesus brings up when inviting people. Though he's endlessly creative, the themes that keep recurring are "repentance" and "the kingdom of God."[3]

I thought I knew about the repentance part (I didn't fully get it, as I'll share later), but the "kingdom of God" part intrigued me. I'd read quite a bit about it during my days in seminary, but I need to confess it mostly didn't stick because the overwhelming theme I remember being taught was that the kingdom would come later, when Jesus returns. I wrongly concluded that, based on its future arrival, I didn't need to worry about it right now.

Jesus' recurring use of the term and others like it got me thinking that perhaps it was worth investigating, and so I started looking through the Bible to understand what the world might look like if God were in charge. What I found astonished me.

A SUBJECT FOR MY CANVAS: MR. ISAIAH

I packed my Bible with a sandwich and drove to the west side of the island to watch the sun set and maybe see some whales while I read the book of Isaiah in a single sitting. The exercise blew my mind. I came to discover that Isaiah had a lot to say about what the world will look like with God in charge. Right at the start is a stunning picture of hope:

Now it will come about that in the last days the mountain of the house of the LORD will be established as the chief of the mountains, and will be raised above the hills; and all the nations will stream to it. And many peoples will come and say, "Come, let us go up to the mountain of the LORD, to the house of the God of Jacob; that He may teach us concerning His ways and that we may walk in His paths." For the law will go forth from Zion and the word of the LORD from Jerusalem. And he will judge between the nations, and will render decisions for many peoples; and they will hammer their swords into plowshares and their spears into pruning hooks. Nation will not lift up sword against nation, and never again will they learn war.[4]

I close my eyes and try to picture it. Leaders from warring nations are joining hands and ascending the mountain of God together because they've been smitten by his beauty and power, his love and justice. They want to learn his ways and when they do, he renders just decisions and reconciles enemies. Then, freed from fear, they destroy their weapons. Picture the Hutus and Tutsis of Rwanda streaming up the mountain, or slaves and slave owners, or apartheid victims and perpetrators, or sexual victims and abusers. They're streaming up the mountain together in pursuit of God, to learn of his ways and walk in his truth. When they descend from the same mountain, they're changed. The hatred the victims had has become forgiveness. The arrogance of the perpetrators has become confession. There's been truthtelling, justice, and healing, all served up with infinite wisdom by the Prince of Peace, who loves all parties.

At the UN building in New York City is a statue, based on this text, of swords being converted into tools of agriculture. The gap, however, between the ideals portrayed by the statue and the realities portrayed in the news is enormous. Peace, it seems, just doesn't happen. Oh sure, we try. Enemies eventually come to the table. Negotiations occur. Treaties are signed.

Then war breaks out again, and the agreements are vaporized in the flames of weapons and broken promises. It's the sad song repeated like a broken record.

Isaiah, though, tells us this won't last forever; eventually peace *will* happen. Theologians debate the when and the how all the time, but they agree on this: when God is reigning fully, there will be peace on earth. And that's just the beginning. The same prophet talks about all the nations coming together, bound under the single peaceful reign of Christ.[5]

He speaks of environmental restoration in ways we can't even fathom.[6] I look to the west, across the waters of Puget Sound to Vancouver Island, and ponder the fact that I live among whales, salmon, and eagles. I came home from coaching one day and watched two bald eagles mating, though at that time I thought it was an aerial war between two adversaries (sex is always so intense!). When they were done, one lay resting in the field. Thinking it was killed in action, I walked out to get a closer look. It took off directly toward me, and I fell down in terror as his giant frame flew away. I ran home shaking, awestruck. What a glorious world, full of diverse, stunning creatures.

On this spectacular island people care about preserving species, care about biodiversity, and well they should, for it is increasingly clear that the well-being of the one is tied to the well-being of the whole. What a tremendous revelation to learn that when God reigns, the biodiversity will be cared for, and this groaning earth will itself be healed.[7]

Isaiah speaks of celebrations and justice, of long life and health. In a world rife with oppression and legalized theft, "They will build houses and inhabit them. They will also plant vineyards and eat their fruit. They will not build and another inhabit. They will not plant and another eat."[8] This reign, I came to discover, is full of beauty and hope. I'd found the subject for my canvas: the good reign of God as portrayed by Isaiah.

As I circled back to the New Testament, I came to discover Jesus reinforced the ethics of which Isaiah spoke. Though he did so all the time, his teachings about this are most clearly crystallized in his Sermon on the Mount. It's there he speaks of reconciling with enemies and loving them, of practicing preemptive forgiveness, of living generously out from spacious and pure hearts. This is the kind of living God's people will do when Christ reigns fully, and the only word I can use to describe it is *stunning*.

The sun was setting, painting the clouds to the west, with shafts of light piercing the veil, so that the ocean was a shimmering field of diamonds, dancing as the wind kissed the waves. Once again, the splendor was overwhelming, and I prayed, grateful for this hint, in this present time, of the glorious beauty that will saturate the cosmos someday, when God restores all things and crushes evil utterly. This is the message I'd been looking for, the hope I'd wanted to impart. This was the subject for the picture I'm called to paint.

FAIR ENOUGH IS NOT FAR ENOUGH

The island fair was coming, and I decided to test the message. Our little church rented a booth and with the help of an artist friend I tried to articulate the good news of Christ's reign in a way that would start conversations with my so-called New Age friends. Stealing a little bit from John Lennon, I asked people to imagine a world where there was no war or tribalism, no oppression or theft, no hunger or disease. I asked people to imagine weapons melting into tools of agriculture, celebration and hospitality displacing fear and isolation.

All of this was on the cover of the pamphlet, along with some great art. When people opened it, the left side had nothing but these Scriptures from Isaiah, as a means of saying, "Look at this! The things you want are the very things that God wants."

On the right side, there were some verses about receiving Christ as Savior, and warnings about the great deception that will come when the Antichrist offers people a counterfeit version of God's reign, without God.

I was thrilled with this little publication, convinced that as soon as people saw what God was about, they'd want to get in on it. I was at the booth when the doors to the fair opened, and as the people walked through the gates for this long-awaited annual event, I was ready. Bible in hand, I simply waited for the harvest.

It never came. Lots of people stopped by and read, but as soon as they saw the Bible verses, most walked away without making any comments at all. In my defensiveness, I built the case that "many are called but few are chosen" and that the seed will fall on all kinds of soil, but there won't be much fruit, so don't sweat it if nobody is listening; it only proves that you're being faithful.[9] Taken to its extreme, of course, this might mean the fewer people that respond, the better.[10]

As the fair was winding down, though, a particular encounter revealed the source of complacency and resistance so many had shown. It became a seed of sorts, planted deep down into the soil of my heart, there to rest fallow until it germinated years later. A thoughtful gentleman approached our table and picked up the pamphlet. He began reading and, instead of a quick dismissal, when he found the punch lines from Isaiah, he found a table and sat down. I watched as he read the whole thing, the fair's horse show competition unfolding behind him as a backdrop.

When he finished, he stood up and came back to speak with me. "This is tremendous material," he said. "I had no idea God was about any of these things." I was busy congratulating myself and getting ready to close the deal and lead him to receive Christ when he said, "So Isaiah talks about people getting to live in their own houses. What is your church doing to address the problem of affordable housing?" Oops. I wasn't expecting that question. "The Bible talks about environmental restoration and justice for the poor? I never knew that! Is your church involved in helping keep the oceans clean, or feeding the hungry? Which of these things Isaiah talks about are you guys doing, because this stuff is exciting!" I think he genuinely wanted to know, but I genuinely had nothing to say. Yes, we occasionally helped a single mom in need, or gave food to someone who'd lost their job, but nothing we were doing looked remotely like the lifestyle of Jesus or God's good reign as portrayed in Isaiah.

We didn't do "kingdom stuff." We did "getting people saved stuff," which had to do with helping people see their failures and sin and understand Christ's death as a solution for that. As I'll share later, the problem wasn't that what we did was wrong but that it was just part of the story, like telling someone about a great baseball game but quitting after a marvelous description of the pitcher putting on his uniform. Our collective fixation on justification and being made right with God has sometimes had the effect of clouding out the grand plan God has for a restored heaven and earth, where nothing is left untouched by the glory, beauty, and healing power of Christ. As a result the subject for the canvas has often been, to say the least, uninspiring.

Looking back, it's clear I was starting to catch a vision for what it means to embody hope, but it was still just a vision, as if I'd seen it in my head but hadn't yet started painting. Nothing on my calendar reflected the priorities Isaiah tells us God envisions. I'll try to address some of the reasons for that in the next chapter, but the truth is I was preaching, praying, baptizing, and leading people to Christ, all without giving Isaiah's vision of God's reign any consideration at all.

"The kingdom? That's for later." With these comforting words, I'd emasculated the gospel into irrelevance, a sin for which I would come to repent.

GETTING IN THE ARENA

Things changed when I moved to the city. I'd continued to wrestle with these questions and was increasingly convinced that the subject matter we're called to paint on the canvas of this world is the hope found in God's good reign. I'd shared with the people who were interviewing me for a new pastorate that my "vision" for the church was nothing other than being the presence of Jesus in Seattle. I explained that this would happen not because of my vision but because God would move people to get involved in making Jesus visible based on their unique gifts and callings. They'd catch a vision of God's good reign and see some way of making it visible, and they'd jump in.

Shortly after my arrival at my new post, I preached a sermon called "Ministry Glasses" in which I encouraged people to see with the eyes of Christ. This included learning to see both the canvas of this world, as we enter fully into it, and the subject we're called to paint, which is the reality of God's reign made visible.

Several weeks after the sermon some people expressed their desire to get involved in a ministry caring for people who were dying of AIDS by taking them to medical appointments, sharing meals, and generally supporting them with friendship so that they didn't need to walk through their valleys alone. We did it, and one of the men who was dying shared his testimony during a Thanksgiving Eve service. There wasn't a dry eye anywhere as he connected the love he'd been shown by Christ's followers with his own decision to follow Jesus. This was the first of many ministries to find expression in our community as a result of people seeing their world through the eyes of Christ and finding their unique ways of contributing to making his life visible.

Since that time, we've welcomed refugees from Sudan and helped them settle. Our church has an active food bank, a homeless shelter, and emerging partnerships with other churches to host community meals for people on the margins. There's a wilderness ministry that includes not only taking people out into creation to encounter hints of God's goodness and beauty, but also includes dialogues and teachings about earth stewardship, partnerships with environmental groups, and trips to Romania to teach low-impact wilderness use. People with medical skills have brought healing in Jesus' name. Others have built houses, dug wells, served in orphanages, cooked meals, given rides to people lacking transportation, and on and on it goes. We're also doing some things together as a community, with everyone involved, as I'll share later.

This is God's good reign made visible. As we continue to wrestle with understanding what it means to be the presence of Jesus in Seattle, God continues to bring clarity to our understanding, and people continue stepping to the front of the line with passion and calling to paint the colors of hope, uniquely, through the gifts God has given them.

I'm reworking the pamphlet I wrote twenty-five years ago, shaping it for a new millennium because I still believe that the message of Isaiah is a marvelous front door for inviting people into God's work in the world. This time, though, when the thoughtful reader asks what our church is doing, I'll be able to smile and say, "Come and see," because the reign of Christ is visible right here, right now.

If the subject is that glorious and beautiful, why aren't all Christ's followers painting hope? There are many reasons, but perhaps the largest is that we think the canvas, which is this world, is about to go up in flames. Is it, and if so, what does that mean for us? I'm glad you asked, because that's where we're going next.

OWN OR RENT

Gaining Perspective

What you do in the present—by painting, preaching, singing, sewing, praying, teaching, building hospitals, digging wells, campaigning for justice, writing poems, caring for the needy, loving your neighbor as yourself—will last into God's future.[1]

    –N. T. WRIGHT

Wherever you are, be all there.

    –JIM ELLIOT

GETTING SAVED: RENTAL STYLE

"Reverend Wilson" is what we called him, and he looked a lot like the guy who was behind the curtain in Oz—white hair, jovial, confident of the truths he proclaimed. Like the man behind the curtain, one of his specialties was helping all of us find our way home. Like Dorothy, we were all lost, he told us, and there was a way back to where we belonged. But we weren't lost in Oz. We were lost in the land called Sin, and the way out wasn't to click our heels together and say, "There's no place like home." It was to receive Christ, which meant admitting you were lost in your own selfishness and looking to Christ for both forgiveness and a way out, a way to live differently, a way home.

All this was meaningless for me as I sat and heard variations on this theme during my childhood. I'd sit quietly and doodle on the bulletin, occasionally glancing at my watch to see if freedom was near or far. One particular Sunday, though, when I was twelve, something strange happened: I listened. What Rev. Wilson was saying made sense. There'd been a growing sense of unease inside me. There were swearing contests at school, with kids competing to see who could use the most profanity during lunch. I didn't win, but it was close. And I'd been sent to the principal's office for telling jokes and getting everyone to laugh uproariously during the quiet study hour. I'd had increasing conflicts with my parents. There were other issues too, all stirring in my soul, so when Rev. Wilson talked that morning about being lost, I knew he was talking to me. He invited anyone who wanted to "find their way home to Jesus" to come forward and pray with him. Sweating and afraid, I knew I needed to do just that. I received Christ and was baptized two weeks later, on Easter Sunday.

> It is a trustworthy statement, deserving full accep-
> tance, that Christ Jesus came into the world to save sinners,
> among whom I am foremost of all.[2]

I hope you didn't think that by comparing Rev. Wilson with the guy from Oz I was implying Jesus is any sort of fairy tale. Finding my way home, beginning that day, was an important foundation for me, and for all who want to live in God's story. It's vital that this foundation remain because, as Peter said, "There is no other name under heaven given among men by which we must be saved."[3] We've got problems. Christ has solutions, and all solutions begin with, and flow out from, relationship with him. Old-school words like *sinners* and *saved* are in the lexicon of faith because, without them, our message quickly mutates into something other than Jesus' and Paul's good news. Before the Christian life is a moral construct or ethical system, it is, first of all, a relationship.[4]

People are abandoning basic truths left and right these days in search of new kinds of Christianity, but I'm increasingly convinced that our problem isn't these foundational truths; it's that these truths have been preached over and over, without telling us the rest of the story.

NOW WHAT?

Soon after receiving Christ and being baptized, I developed a problem. Though I kept showing up and listening, the invitation to get saved was the only message I heard, Sunday after Sunday. I'd sit there in church, but by the time I was fourteen I was ready for something more, some sort of "next step" beyond this promise of finding my way home, which I'd understood to mean finding my way to heaven and avoiding hell in the process. I was still waiting to hear that next step when I moved away and left the church behind for a while. I was convinced attending worship services each weekend was sort of like being given the ingredients to cook an endless variety of recipes but taught to cook the same dish, over and over again, every week for eighteen years. Eventually, you crave something more, or at least something different.

The reality is the same ingredients that change our destiny can be used in an almost infinite variety of ways to offer tasteful, life-giving food to our broken and hungry world. This is how we're invited to impart blessing. Jesus exemplified this in both his teaching and living. The ingredients of reconciliation and justification, so often the centerpiece of churches and theologians, are more like the basic ingredients; you can't cook without them, but the flavors that flow from them, like hospitality, service, and solidarity with the downtrodden, will create artistic food through which we'll be able to love and bless the world. The early church embodied this ethic, living differently than the prevailing culture so that the life-giving food that is Jesus' life could be experienced and shared.

"Living differently," however, wasn't on the radar for many Christians during my childhood, with the exception perhaps of calling people to superficial differences like length of hair and manner of dress, with a nod thrown in for sexual purity. In some parts of the country, you could sing hymns wearing your Sunday best the morning after wearing the cloth of the Klan on Saturday night. Caring for the environment wasn't even a subject yet, except among some fringe "pagans" who were sounding the alarm that our pesticides were killing birds and lakes and would eventually start killing us too.

In those tumultuous sixties it seems many in the church looked at the protesters and pushers as nothing more than losers who needed Jesus, the tacit understanding being that when they came to Christ they'd put a tie on, or at least shoes, start going to church, and embrace the American Dream. Wrestling with questions about justice, racial reconciliation, and "just war" weren't in the purview of the Christians I knew, and questions of acid rain and chemical pollution affecting fertility were the concerns of what we called the "unchurched," because (poor souls) this world was all they had.

TENANT OR OWNER

We who knew Christ, on the other hand, were taught that our time here on earth is short, that our real interests need to be spiritual, not physical—the things of heaven rather than earth. The hymns we sang declared this ("This world is not my home, I'm just a passin' through"), reinforcing the preaching that was offered up week after week. I learned that my relationship with this world was similar to that of a tenant to a landlord. We're here for now, but we've no long-term vested interest in the world, the earth, or anything in it.

When I was attending seminary, my wife and I rented an apartment, a simple place we chose because it was quiet and had a pool. It was occupied mostly by retirees, some of them Jewish, which was nice because one of them helped me study Hebrew. We enjoyed our days there, close to shopping, work, and school. On hot days we'd jump in the pool at night to cool off and crawl into bed hoping to fall asleep before we became dry and hot.

We were definitely *tenants*. The truth is that while we lived there, we did care about the place to some extent: we cleaned the stove, vacuumed the carpets, and even occasionally washed the windows. But major improvements or repairs? Forget it. We were renters. So when the air-conditioner didn't work, and the ceiling was so poorly insulated that on one really warm day it got hot enough in our apartment to melt candles, causing them to bend over like prostrate sun worshipers, none of this was our problem. We'd complain, but whether things got better or not, finding solutions was neither our responsibility nor our expense. We were renters, and so ultimately, broken things weren't worth the investment because we weren't fully invested there.

The theological counterpart to this mindset is what I call Rental Theology. This has the effect of dividing our reality into two worlds: the stuff we care about and the stuff we don't. The stuff rental Christians care about is the stuff we'll have forever, which, in this paradigm, is generally the invisible stuff: our spirits, our personalities in some form, and our relationship with God. There might be a few more things added to the list, depending on nuances, but essentially, rental theology says we own the invisible stuff, and we rent the stuff you can taste, touch, feel.

If we're renters, the "inner life" should occupy the major investment of our time and attention. *If we're renters.* Are we?

WHOSE EARTH IS IT, ANYWAY?

I understand why people would think someone else owns the place. The seemingly endless boatloads of suffering and oppression have many thinking that God's simply given up on this planet. One of the misunderstandings that lead to this conclusion comes from the way some of the biblical authors use the words *world* and *earth*. John says, "Do not love the world nor the things in the world. If anyone loves the world, the love of the Father is not in him."[5] Or, as Paul puts it: "Set your mind on the things above, not on things that are on earth."[6]

Seems clear enough, doesn't it? Most of my Bible teachers thought so, all the way through graduate school. Over and over again it was implied, if not explicitly stated, that this world is in the firm grip of Satan, and God has only one thing in mind for it: total destruction. If this is true, then nothing matters, literally nothing at all, except preparing people for their eternal destination. Bible study trumps going to a concert every time. In fact, this worldview might lead you to rejoice every time there's a new war or earthquake, because that's a sign God's about to destroy everything and bring this ugly history to an end, ushering the saved into a state of eternal bliss.

I heard this all the time, but because I enjoyed reading the Bible, I kept running into other passages that *didn't* fit this scheme. David tells us "the earth is the LORD's, and all it contains."[7] God hasn't handed it over to evil forces, or raised a surrender flag while sneakily planning a global firestorm so he still wins in the end. He's the *owner*; patiently and carefully he's working things out toward the day when all things will be made new.

Further, we're told in Romans 8 that this created world is longing for humanity's redemption, because when we're fully restored, creation itself will be fully restored. Let's not forget the imagery of Isaiah, which paints a picture of stunning beauty, a world saturated with justice, celebration, forgiveness, and healing. Far from checking out, it seems God is heavily invested.

There's more. Those who have joined in God's story have joined more than a story; they've joined a family. The language the Bible uses to describe this is remarkable. We're called "heirs with Christ,"[8] and "He is not ashamed to call [us] brothers."[9] When we come to Christ, we become part of his family, meaning that *the earth isn't just the Lord's; it's ours too.* This makes sense, because it was given to us in the first place to steward and subdue, back when God created it. "The meek," we're told, "will inherit the earth."[10] Where's the value in such an inheritance if the earth is just a stinking orb of evil, destined for utter destruction after the faithful have been plucked off?

Yes, it's true that the "world system" is filled with destructive mindsets, longings, and ideologies. John calls them "lust" and "pride,"[11] both of which are at the root of ugliness and suffering. This lustful and pride-filled world is the world that is "in the power of the evil one,"[12] as John tells us. And it's because of these elements that there's a destruction that's yet to occur, as Peter reminds us,[13] but this is for purification and in order to make "all things new."[14] Still, some people use Peter's words to essentially say that painting hope on the canvas of this world is a waste of time; it all goes in the fire someday. Such fatalism is foolish *and* inconsistent with how we live the rest of our lives.

My wife and I bought a house in Seattle back in 1996. I'm sorry to report it's not going to make it. It was built in 1928 and is leaning downhill a little bit, toward the lake. It's been through a couple of earthquakes, the evidence of which can be seen where the plaster has cracked, making some places look a little tired. It may be a while, but someday an earthquake, or fire, or investor, or war, or neglect will spell the end of this old house. Despite the gloomy future reality, however, we've been improving it now for fifteen years: new paint and siding on the outside, new deck, vegetable garden, inside paint, and, because we love forests, the planting of two firs, a California redwood, two vine maples, two cedars, and a hemlock in our backyard. Now we live in the midst of evergreens, our favorite kind of cathedral, even though the house won't last forever.

In the same way our house benefited from new siding, the needs of our broken world benefit from justice and mercy done in Jesus' name. We planted a garden in the backyard and made a shelter for birds, fully knowing even the trees we planted will be gone someday. There's value in *this* moment, *this* beauty, *this* justice, *this* hospitality. That's what Jesus taught us when he told us to be a mustard seed of hope, a yeast flake of redemption.[15] He said God's good reign, which will come in fullness someday, is here already, present in small ways through the lives of the faithful. Don't worry about when the end will come; get on with being the presence of the future right here, right now. You'll inherit the earth, according to Jesus, so why not paint hope on it today?

FROM PURVEYORS OF INFORMATION TO ARTISTS OF HOPE

Our calling, like that of Jesus when he walked on the earth, is to beautify, with splashes of kingdom color. This means we'll need to have a sense of what the kingdom colors are, and then learn from Christ, the Master Artist, what it means to paint those colors onto the grey canvas of our broken world. Learning about these colors and how to paint with them is a big part of what the church calls *discipleship*. It's what Jesus taught his disciples to do both through his words and his example.

Look, there's a splash of reconciliation as Jesus breaks down social walls that divide according to race and gender. He's talking with a Samaritan woman. He continues painting by imparting his invitation to new life, offering the power to overcome her penchant for failed relationships.

There he is, standing in the temple among those devoted to the rituals of worship and shouting an invitation to "anyone who is thirsty."[16] These people knew about thirst, living in their arid land and walking hot and dusty roads to village wells for life-sustaining water. Every step toward the well is one step closer to a satisfaction that can be met by nothing other than water. Acquiring it becomes a singular obsession for those in need.

Thirsty? Yes. Perhaps they were thirsty for freedom as they were finding themselves under the thumb of yet another occupying political power, wondering if they'd ever recover their national identity. Maybe some among the crowd were thirsty for meaning, for healing, for strength. But whatever they were thirsting for, Jesus made the audacious claim that if people would simply come to him (there's that altar-call piece that opened our conversation), they'd not only find their own thirst quenched, they'd become rivers themselves! He's painting meaning, intimacy, and satisfaction onto the canvas.

There's a woman, about to be stoned to death, guilty of adultery. Jesus again paints over shame and condemnation, exposing them to be forgeries of kingdom colors, seeking legitimacy under the banner of religion. He uses the color of forgiveness instead, but not without including the color of transformation, as he invites her to "go and sin no more."[17]

John tells us there are so many colors on Jesus' palette the Gospel writers didn't have enough space to declare them all. Jesus did take care, though, to make it clear our calling is to follow in his footsteps as artisans of hope. He told his disciples, explicitly, to go into the world and declare that the kingdom of God had come, and to show the reality of God's new reign by spilling the colors of hope across our world's canvas. "Heal the sick. . . . Freely you have received. Freely give."[18] Then, before leaving, he said it all again, reminding us to teach people to become followers of Jesus, artists in the same way he is an artist, which is different than simply receiving Jesus as a Savior to save us from hell.[19]

Like the Gospel writers, I've not enough time to talk about all the ways and places where people are spilling hope, but here are a few. Curtis is helping put an end to human trafficking through his band, Jubilee. Doru is raising up a new generation of business leaders in Romania. All over the globe people are living out their calling as artists, painting vibrant colors. They inspire me to live in God's story. They remind me that unless we're intentional about embracing our calling as artisans of hope, we've not yet fully entered into our calling as followers of Christ.

This has changed my world utterly. Before coming to this understanding of my calling as an artist, I'd thought giving people information about God, Jesus, and the depravity of the human condition was the extent of my calling. Yes, these three things are important. The road I'm on still sees humanity as sinful, still sees Christ's death and resurrection as central and foundational. The difference is this: When I discovered that I'm a co-owner with Christ, that I'm the citizen of a kingdom he's creating, I learned I'm to do more than call people to find a way out of hell. I'm to make God's good reign visible on this earth and invite others to do the same.

FROM CONFRONTATION TO INVITATION

Our church took this "artisans of hope" theme and ran with it a couple of years ago, as we invited people, on Easter

Sunday, to step into God's story and spill hope onto the canvas of God's beautiful and broken world. We challenged people to spend the fifty days between Easter and Pentecost painting the colors of justice, liberation, and healing in Jesus' name. By committing to simplifying our lives to the tune of $1 a day, and giving that money or more, we were able to raise $132,000 for wells in Uganda. We had so much fun the first year, we did it again. Now the Spilling Hope initiative is available nationally for churches and individuals.[20] This is a way of saying, "Christ's reign of justice, mercy, generosity, has begun. His triumph over death has inaugurated a new regime of hope. Come join the story God is writing!"

We need to invite people to be reconciled to Jesus so that we can invite them into their calling. Reconciliation without participation just doesn't work, because it's like getting a set of paints and brushes while never getting to do art.

"Rental Theology" makes painting appear to be a waste of time. According to some of today's popular Bible teachers, we've already received our foreclosure papers, and we'll be moving soon. (Around 2012 is the most recent prediction, though I've heard 1977, 1978, 1987, 1988, 1993, 2000, 2001, and 2003 in my short lifetime; each was the year it was supposed to end. Suffice to say I've stopped holding my breath.) Transferring all our hope to the future and removing any hint of God's reign from the present puts a wet blanket on the artisan's soul before he or she even has a chance to begin. We've been taught that our contribution to the canvas is, at best, incidental, at worst a waste of time. It's tragic, and it's not the real gospel.

If Jesus returns before this book gets published, I hope he finds me using the gifts he's given me to bless the world. I hope he finds me being an artist, painting hope in my unique way. I hope he finds my church doing that too, collectively.

In Jesus' kingdom everyone's an artist. Everyone.

PART TWO

THE PRIMARY COLORS

I'm writing this as I stare out the window of a log cabin hidden in the foothills of Washington State's Cascades, near skiing, climbing, and the ocean, all at the same time. The beauty of the place can be summarized by the word *green*, though the word doesn't do it justice, because there are so many shades. There's the green that is the moss growing on the stump of a fir that was downed years ago to make this log cabin. There's the green shoots from the tulips just breaking through the earth, along with the skunk cabbage, blue spruce, and mysterious ground cover that carpets the forest floor. Each green has variations, shades created by light and dark, sun and shadow. Counting the greens is like counting stars.

Try painting this kaleidoscope of color, if you dare. Those who can have tapped into the mystery of primary colors, of which there are only three: blue, red, and yellow. This seems like nonsense here in the Evergreen State, here in the cabin surrounded with a thousand shades of green, and a sky that's grey enough, often enough, that the word *blue* is declared only by faith. "Ah," says my artist friend, "all those greens, in their various shades, are just blends of blue and yellow. There are infinite shades of green, but each is nothing more than a blend."

She goes on to tell me that red, blue, and yellow are the three colors from which all colors derive. I continue to listen, but behind the curtain of polite attention, my mind has gone theological, as I ponder the complexity of God's laws in Israel;

ten commandments, which, in the hands of scholars, became 613 interpretations, which then spawned volumes and schools of thought. The complexity of it can get a little overwhelming. I wish the obtuse and multifaceted nature of what God is calling us toward could, like colors, be reduced down to three "primary colors" from which all God's ethics, and priorities, and plans could be derived. Then I remember:

> He has told you, O man, what is good; and what does
> the LORD require of you but to do justice, to love kindness,
> and to walk humbly with your God?[1]

"All the colors are a blend of these three," my artist friend says, her words calling me back to the present for an instant. I ponder the reality that marriages healed, wells dug, schools and hospitals built, generosity practiced, weapons laid down in the pursuit of reconciliation, apartheid ended, literacy increased, mentorships begun, homeless folks sheltered, meals cooked, toilets cleaned—all are various blends of the principles here in Micah 6:8. Every act of beauty carried out in Christ's name derives from a blend of these, God's three primary colors.

In this world where daily we hear voices competing for our loyalties and the investment of our time, money, and emotions, it's profoundly encouraging to know that God has boiled it down. God has made it simple. God has given us three colors to acquire and nurture: justice, mercy, intimacy with him.

Everything good and beautiful, hopeful and life-giving, joyful and wise will be created by blending these colors. Knowing them and learning how to blend them together are what enable us to fulfill our calling as artisans of hope. Let's get started.

DO JUSTICE
The Horrible Sounds of Silence

*Justice in the life and conduct of the State is possible only as
first it resides in the hearts and souls of the citizens.*

—PLATO

*This is the kind of fast day I'm after: to break the chains of
injustice, get rid of exploitation in the workplace, free the
oppressed, cancel debts. What I'm interested in seeing you do
is: sharing your food with the hungry, inviting the homeless poor
into your homes, putting clothes on the shivering ill-clad, being
available to your own families.*[1]

—ISAIAH 58:6–7

In 1993 I traveled to India for the first time, and the journey,
more than the destination, revealed the absence of the justice
color on my palette. The trip was long and complex: Vancouver
to Hong Kong; overnight stay; Hong Kong to Bangkok; Bangkok
to Delhi. There my friend would pick me up and we'd drive six

hours north into the Himalayan foothills to the Bible school where I'd be teaching.

I'd landed in Bangkok and was awaiting a late evening flight to Delhi on Aeroflot, a Russian airline. I'm reading my ticket and looking up at the board, realizing that the destination of my flight number says Moscow. This is troubling to me, the more so as I look around the area where people are waiting to check in. Everyone looks Russian or, at the very least, utterly Caucasian. The check-in area isn't open yet, so I've no one to speak with, but a sense of unease grows with the appearance of each waiting passenger. I build a scenario in my mind to comfort myself: *Maybe we're an entire flight of Russian-speaking white people who are planning on going to India. Maybe the reader board has it wrong. Yes, that's it; the reader board is wrong.* I look at my ticket and confirm the flight number. It's January, and all the passengers have warm coats out, even though it was over 90° in Bangkok that day and over 80° in Delhi. *We're going to Delhi,* I assure myself, quickly becoming the poster-child for irrationality and denial.

A woman opens the counter and I wait, nervously. Finally I hand her my ticket; she looks at it and says *nyet* before declaring in broken English that, yes, I do have a seat on this plane, and yes, this is the flight number. But "if you board," she says, "you'll be going all the way to Moscow. The plane only stops in Delhi for fuel. You can't get off there." She stares at me coldly, and I ask her what I should do. She ignores my question, looks at the person behind me, and begins speaking in Russian, her body language pushing me out of the line.

I'm standing in the airport clueless regarding what to do next. I call my contact in Canada and tell him to fax my friend in India and let him know I'm delayed. He, a seasoned traveler, suggests I check with the airline responsible for all the other legs of my flight and see what they can do to help. I find their office, which thankfully is still open, as it's getting late into the evening. A woman looks at my ticket, types into her computer, and says, "This flight would have taken you to Moscow."

"This is the problem," I say. "I want to go to Delhi."

She types for what seems like forever, then says, "I can put you on stand-by for a flight to Delhi that leaves tomorrow night." With this news, I feel the anxiety drain from my body. I ask her where I should stay and she says, "There's a list of hotels on a board by the main entrance. Write down the number of the one you choose and give it to a cab outside. They'll take care of you."

After perusing the board, I settle on a $30 room, walk outside, and hand the hotel number to the first cab driver I see. As we journey through the city, the friendly driver tells me he knows of a cheaper hotel that's closer to the airport and even better than the one I've chosen. When he tells me the price, I do the math in my head: $21! "Let's do it," I say, proud of my thrift and good fortune to find such a helpful driver.

We drive for at least ten more minutes, and he reminds me to use condoms. I wonder what he's talking about and tell him my wife and I have other birth control methods. He laughs. "Not your wife," he says. "Your girls here in Bangkok. Use condoms. Lots of disease, man—lots of disease." As we pull into the motel parking lot I assure him I love my wife and won't be visiting any Bangkok girls. He laughs and, as he pulls away, shouts through the window, "Use condoms!"

The neighborhood doesn't look very good, but what can you expect for $21? The adjacent karaoke bar has loud music blasting through the open doors and barking dogs running in and out. I enter a lobby covered in gauche red carpet and cheap furniture, but like I said, it's $21. After running my credit card, the manager calls the bellhop, who hoists my backpack and leads me upstairs to my room.

The lobby, it turns out, was the most tasteful part of the place. We wander down a hallway that looks like something out of a prison movie; grey concrete walls, grey floor, grey metal doors. The bellhop opens my door and gives me the quick tour: "Here's the air-conditioner," he says, proudly showing me how it can be turned on, or off, whichever I choose! "Here's the shower," he says, demonstrating it too. "Of course, the bed," he says, "with clean sheets tonight!" (I can only presume there's a grammar slip here, that something's being lost in translation.)

I thank him for the tour, and he remains. I give him a tip; he smiles and says, "Thank you, sir. Now, when would you like the girl?" I assume I've heard him wrong, and my mind runs through its vocabulary Rolodex looking for what other words sound like *girl*. "When would you like the . . . what? The *call* (a wake-up call?); the *roll* (for breakfast, maybe?); the *grill* (a midnight BBQ?).

"Excuse me?" I say, prompting clarification. With his accent I thought he said *girl*.

"There's a girl that comes with the room. Very nice. Very young. She can come now or later. You let me know. You have condoms?"

I begin to feel sick to my stomach. I pull out my wallet and show him pictures of my wife and children. "Very pretty," he says. "Now, when would you like the girl?" He's getting impatient.

"I'd like the girl to stay out of my room," I say, and he protests that she comes with the room. When I insist, he tells me the room will cost the same, even if she doesn't come. I nearly gag and tell him I'm leaving. He looks frustrated. "No refunds," he says as we walk back to the lobby.

There's a girl walking down the hall as we leave, wearing a dress that hugs every curve. She's got high heels, thick shadow framing her hollow eyes. She looks to be all of seventeen. The hallway starts spinning as I feel visceral reactions of rage, fear, and powerlessness coursing through my body. What's going on here? I want to kill the desk clerk but instead ask him to call for a cab. Within an hour, I'm on the airport floor, trying to sleep off the nightmare I've just experienced.

Sleep is the wrong word, because what's just happened is that I've peered through this window of injustice for the first time, and what I've seen has shaken me to the core. I felt helpless, but more significantly, felt that my work, my teaching, and my faith were all utterly disconnected with what I'd just seen. It's one thing to tell people, because they love Jesus, not to sleep with prostitutes. It's another thing entirely to attack the systemic issues of poverty and debt that would compel a family to sell their teenage daughter for the price of a Happy Meal, with the result that she might sleep with up to twenty men a night.[2] Does God care about these systemic issues, and the oppression that flows from them? Does he want us to address them, or is it enough that we'll go to heaven someday? Welcome to "doing justice."

THE COLOR OF JUSTICE

Isaiah is a master at exposing what Richard Stearns has called "the hole in our gospel."[3] The prophet talks about how God has grown tired of people singing and bringing offerings.[4] He says a lot of people are wearing the outward clothes of holiness but failing to really live in ways that honor God and reveal his character. They're going to church, worshiping, praying, all the typical things that make people stand up and take notice of someone's religious depth. But something's missing.

Later,[5] the people are trying to understand why they're disconnected to God. They're seeking God day by day. They're delighting in learning about his ways. They're spiritual; they're involved in religious rituals; they're devout. And something's missing.

You can change the details, but this is the story of the ages. Faith becomes institutionalized, and the means of seeking God becomes formalized. Soon we who are called "spiritual leaders" are teaching people how to do the things good Christians do: read your Bible, pray, have a personal relationship with Jesus, tell others about Christ. Maybe if we really go deep with people, we equip them to defend their faith, discover their spiritual gifts, get their financial house in order, and stay married (or celibate, if they're single). We can do all this—diligently, and still, if we're honest, feel disconnected with God, as if something's missing.

Something *is* missing: *the point of it all!*

Jesus began his public ministry by taking his turn to read in the synagogue of Nazareth. He opens the scroll on what, to all appearances, would be just another Sabbath for those in attendance, and begins to read, from the Isaiah scroll:

> "The Spirit of the Lord is upon me, because He anointed me to preach the gospel to the poor. He has sent me to proclaim release to the captives, and recovery of sight to the blind, to set free those who are oppressed, to proclaim the favorable year of the Lord."[6]

What happens next is off the map. Everyone's waiting for the next element in the "order of worship," but Jesus remains standing, looking around the room until everyone's eyes are fixed on him. There's this awkward silence until he speaks again:

> "Today this Scripture has been fulfilled in your hearing."[7]

If he'd only stopped there, all would have been well. He was popular at that moment, and the oppressed Jews of Nazareth no doubt interpreted what he'd just said as meaning the Messiah would be turning the tables, and it would be the Gentiles' turn to be enslaved and oppressed. Instead, Jesus tells them some Old Testament stories to remind them that God's vision for justice means justice *for everybody*, that the Gentiles aren't God's adversaries, that this new kingdom will reconcile *all* enemies, end *all* oppression, that there'll be *no* outsiders. This kind of justice, reconciling, and forgiveness wasn't what people were looking for in a Messiah, so they tried to push him off a cliff. It wasn't the last time the social implications of the gospel would make people mad at Jesus.

That this was his mission was evident from that day forward. His ministry spoke to the spiritually oppressed (like the man filled with demons) and the physically oppressed (like the prostitute who likely had no other available means of income). He healed the spiritually blind (like the religious leader who couldn't understand the meaning of "born again") and the physically blind. He set people free from captivity to sin and painted the picture of a day yet to come when all people would be set free from every form of captivity. His mission of deliverance was total, and because of this, Jesus was "doing justice" all his days.

Fast-forward to the end of his ministry. When Jesus talks about the end of the ages and judgment day, he tells certain ones to proceed to the right (not a political statement), where they'll inherit God's kingdom. Why will they inherit it? In his words: "I was hungry and you gave me something to eat, I was thirsty and you gave me something to drink, I was a stranger and you invited me in, I needed clothes and you clothed me, I was sick and you looked after me, I was in prison and you came to visit me."[8]

Jesus seems to be saying that real love for God will be seen not in outward shows of religiosity—which were often the gold standard for spirituality when I was young—but in love for, and service to, the poor and disenfranchised of this world. Who knew?

A limited understanding of faith explains why the church actively opposed Martin Luther King Jr. and his nonviolent resistance to racial injustice.[9] You could be at a lynching on Saturday night and singing in the choir on Sunday morning. It explains how the church could be at the forefront—a century earlier—of resisting the end of slavery.[10] It explains how the church could sing loud songs about loving God and their neighbors, and refuse to share their wealth in order to care for children orphaned by AIDS.[11] And it explains how the most Christianized nation in Africa could hack up nearly one million of its own citizens with machetes. They were worshiping together one week, and a few weeks later they were murdering each other, with some of the perpetrators being pastors and priests.[12] Take the commitment to "do justice" off your palette, and religion quickly mutates into something hideous.

No wonder people are turned off. What they're rejecting, though, isn't the vibrant artistry of hope, seen in its countless shades of beauty wherever justice happens in Christ's name. Instead people are rejecting cheap, ugly forgeries. People today declare that they're not interested in a God who is racist, or greedy, or tribal. The good news is that the God of the Bible is deeply committed to justice, and invites us, as his artisans, to "do justice" as a means of making his good reign visible.

That's why the Bible is saturated with this color. Amos spoke of it when he said he'd rather see good justice than good singing.[13] James spoke of it when he said true religion consists in caring for people on the margins.[14] Jesus made this kind of justice his own sort of personal mission statement, as we've already seen, when he quoted Isaiah and said that he'd come to release captives, give sight to the blind, and proclaim the favorable year of the Lord. Debts forgiven, captives set free, downtrodden and oppressed vindicated? The real faith that grows because of Jesus, it turns out, is vibrant and alive with all the beautiful shades that come from this primary color of justice.

This is the color that often seems missing on our palettes; the reality is that if you're reading this book, there's every likelihood that you, along with me, are among the wealthiest 5 percent of people alive. There's also a good chance, with all that wealth, you're using more than your fair share of resources, as I am. The odds are strong, in our collective case, that taking a hard look at what God has to say about justice might change the size of our car, the amount of money we give away and where it goes, even our job.

Who wants to do that? It's far easier to frame the gospel wholly in terms of my spiritual problem and my need to get right with God in order to escape his judgment, with perhaps the added bonus of some inner peace and maybe even economic prosperity tossed in as sort of thank-you gifts from God for choosing Jesus.

The practitioner of this less colorful faith is excused from dealing with justice issues because captivity, oppression, and poverty, all issues in the biblical narrative, aren't viewed as literal; they're spiritualized, so that, for instance, the Exodus story becomes purely a metaphor illustrating how Jesus sets our hearts free from the slavery of sin.[15] A little interpretive sleight of hand and poof! I can be rich, toss a few coins to the poor, and ignore the systemic underlying causes of injustice and oppression.

But then something happens. You pass a seventeen-year-old girl in the hallway of a Bangkok motel, fully knowing that she's selling herself, and you say, "I can't keep pretending I live in Disneyland, singing hymns and practicing personal piety while human trafficking steals children's souls, and thirty thousand people die every day of treatable diseases. I can't continue to live 'faith as usual' when I learn how many billions of people are making the same amount of money in a year that I make in three days." If knowing all this doesn't shake you to the core, something's probably wrong with your view of Jesus and the life to which we're invited.

JUSTICE: FOUND IN TRANSLATION

While living in Los Angeles, my wife and I had some friends working in a halfway house for women who were trying to get out of the prostitution business. Getting out is difficult and dangerous, so they needed to protect their identities. One Sunday, because I had a car, we picked up a couple of them for church. We parked and walked into the enormous sanctuary where thousands of people had their hands raised in worship. Awesome music, awesome devotion, awesome atmosphere. I was just getting into it when one of them said, "We need to leave. Now!" She was loud, angry, intense.

Without asking for clarification, we left and as soon as we were outside she said, "I saw three men worshiping in there who are clients." These women, just beginning to explore Christianity, took a giant step backward that day. No wonder God doesn't always like the singing.

In Isaiah 1, the theme that will unfold again and again is being addressed for the first time. People are doing all the right "worship" things, and God is letting Isaiah know he's not impressed. He's tired of going to church meetings and watching people drop money in the plate. He's tired of pious prayers; even the incense isn't a turn-on. God is bored in church. The reason, of course, is that the people's "hands are covered with blood."[16]

God shows Israel the remedy for this kind of disconnect and hypocrisy. "You want me to worship with you? Then, 'remove the evil of your deeds from My sight. Cease to do evil. Learn to do good; seek justice, reprove the ruthless, defend the orphan, plead for the widow.' "[17] Justice, in other words, is intensely relational. It has to do with finding those on the margins (which, in the day of Isaiah, would have included the widow and the orphan) and addressing the issues keeping them locked out of wholeness.

THE MANY SHADES OF JUSTICE

Donald Miller is not just a bestselling author. He's also the visionary behind "The Mentoring Project,"[18] a group responding to the crisis of fatherlessness in America by inspiring and equipping faith communities to mentor fatherless boys. The absence of the father is a justice issue, and when it's discussed, the left blames our social structures while the right blames the implosion of the family. Nobody, though, blames the children. They're victims. "Doing justice" means strengthening, standing in the gap, and being a father for the fatherless, because that's what God is for us.

Walter Pimpong is a pastor in Ghana. This is a country whose 1992 constitution mandates the end of all slavery and slavelike practices within their borders. Despite this cultural declaration, ancient practices in the region are keeping women and girls, as young as five, as slaves because of a practice called *trokosi*, a word meaning "slave to the gods." Ending the *trokosi* has become a central mission for Walter.

When a crime is committed, the offended party sets a

process into motion that will result in precious lives being held in bondage. As the International Needs website describes it:

> An aggrieved person determines what the crime or offense is and reports it to the shrine priest in order to punish the guilty party's family with mysterious deaths and diseases. It is then that the family is forced to send a young virgin to stop the curses believed to be caused by the Fetish gods. During the humiliating initiation ceremony, the new slave is stripped of any clothing except a cloth between her thighs. She is then paraded through her village.[19]

A typical example of this practice can be found in the story of Abla, a young girl who came into the world because her father raped his own niece. To pay for the crime, the family has given Abla to the local priest, where she'll face mental, physical, and sexual abuse. She does farming chores, hauls water, cooks, and cleans, and in a year or two, she'll become the object of the priest's sexual advances and pleasures. He'll beat her without fear of reprisal when she fails to please him in any way. She'll be denied any access to education and literacy, which will further her dependency on the priest, potentially making her slavery permanent and her life short. There are thousands just like her in Ghana and neighboring regions.

Walter is a pastor. He preaches, teaches, baptizes, and helps people learn how to read and study their Bibles. He trains new pastors in all these things too. He's also working to free women from slavery and developing vocational training resources for them, finding sources of clean water, and building schools where boys and girls will develop literacy skills and learn about Christ. All the colors are on this man's palette, and he's painting pictures of hope in Ghana. To date, at least 3,500 girls have been freed, and laws have been enacted to make trokosi illegal, though it continues to be practiced.[20]

I'm a pastor as well, but I did "pastor things" for nearly a decade without even thinking about "doing justice." What I learned during that decade is that when you only have two colors on your palette, the pictures you create distort God's good news. While Walter is finding children who can't go to school and providing them with a uniform and a daily hot meal, I'm arguing about whether the days in Genesis 1 are literal or figurative. While he's meeting with the fetish priests, befriending them, and buying girls back one at a time, I'm debating whether or not people can still speak in tongues now that God's done writing the Bible. While he's overseeing water projects as a way of creating the foundation for health and education, I'm debating whether Isaiah had one, two, or three authors.

But when the color of justice is thrown into the mix, our faith priorities readjust themselves, and our faith becomes more compelling, more powerful. Learning to see with the eyes of Christ and developing a passion to see God's "kingdom come, his will be done, on earth as it is in heaven," we step into the story that God is writing, feeding the hungry, clothing the naked, addressing systemic issues of oppression, and continuing to learn what the color of justice looks like so that we can apply it generously on the canvas of our grey and hurting world.

Seeing justice is inviting, beautiful, life-imparting, liberating, hopeful. But doing justice is costly because it means stepping outside our often insulated and comfortable lives and pouring ourselves out on behalf of others. That's why, when God lays out the primary colors, he doesn't tell us to find examples of justice, or to study justice, or to talk about justice or watch movies about justice. He tells us to *do* justice.

After visiting Bangkok and getting sick to my stomach, I slowly began spending less time arguing about inerrancy, eschatology, and the temporality or permanence of spiritual gifts, and more time getting on with what God is doing: releasing captives, opening blind eyes, freeing the oppressed, and seeking, in any and every way possible, to embody his good reign by painting hope right in the midst of the places where despair is deepest.

I've a long way to go in learning what doing justice fully means, and even further to go before I can consider what I'm doing exemplary. But I'm definitely on that road: wells in Africa, homeless shelter in Seattle, a community garden in the works—who knows what's next, all through the church I lead, as we "do justice—in Jesus' name." As a result, the pictures of hope I'm painting these days look a lot more like the stuff Jesus spoke of all the time; that makes me excited, and grateful to be in God's story.

Justice alone, though, will never paint the pictures of hope that reflect God's heart. I would soon discover that when the *second* primary color is added, what appears is artistry of such stunning beauty that the only explanation for it is supernatural. It's time to learn about mercy.

MERCY MOUNTAINEERS

The Challenge of Lovingkindness

When you hold resentment toward another, you are bound to that person or condition by an emotional link that is stronger than steel. Forgiveness is the only way to dissolve that link and get free.

–CATHERINE PONDER

Freely you have received . . . freely give.[1]

–JESUS CHRIST

When I'm climbing mountains, there are many moments when my entire world shrinks down to one simple thought: "Take the next step." Once I do that, I determine to take the next step, and then the one after that. Sometimes when I'm climbing up a steep area of snow that requires every last ounce of energy, the only way I can keep going is by playing a little game to distract my mind from how miserable I am. I guess how many steps it is from where I am to my goal, and then I start counting, step by step. I do this because carrying a pack on my back at eight or nine thousand feet takes me to the limit of my capacity.

Guides, though, need capacities beyond that. I remember the first time I climbed Mount Baker, one member of our party lost his ice axe. All of us watched as it slid down the mountain and fell into a crevasse. The guide sat us all down on the glacier, told us not to move, and then descended. Climbing down into the crevasse, he retrieved the axe and then returned to us. As I watched I thought, *I'm glad he has the energy. If I'd have been the guide I'd have said, "You lost your ice axe. You go get it. I need to catch my breath."*

Around this point in grasping the vision for becoming an artisan of hope, I sometimes feel as if Jesus is asking me not to just climb a mountain, but to be a guide. He's told me I'm "blessed to be a blessing,"[2] and that means living larger than merely getting myself up the mountain of maturity. It means serving others, as we've seen, by embodying his kingdom reign of justice, and this takes emotional, spiritual, and even physical energy.

There are days, months even, when I just don't feel like I have it, when I feel it's all I can do to keep climbing, and the thought of helping others feels "over the top." What's behind this sense of being overwhelmed? A spiritual director might start peeking around in my life and attribute it to busyness, saying yes too often, losing my bearings by neglecting intimacy with God (as we'll see in the next chapter).

That's part of it, but for all of us, to varying degrees, there's something else at work: it's our woundedness. Infidelity. Sexual abuse. Physical abuse. Abject neglect. Parents with addictions that destroyed our family. Friends who betrayed us in permanently life-altering ways. Profound losses that came about because of someone's mistreatment. Lots of people are carrying a really heavy pack up the mountain, and it's all they can do to keep going. When they hear sermons about needing to be a blessing, needing to serve, needing to become an artisan of hope, they think: *Let people get their own ice axes. Let people rescue themselves. I'm barely surviving.*

I'm convinced that many people are carrying these gigantic loads around because they've failed to use this second primary color on their palette. We're told to "do justice" and to "love mercy." Mercy can also be translated "lovingkindness," and however you translate it, the truth is that finding a way to let this quality grow inside us is the key to shedding our rucksack full of garbage and hurt. Thus freed, we now have the potential of becoming not just climbing tourists but guides—those strong enough to point the way skyward.

Where in the world can we go to learn about nurturing lovingkindness? How about the home of a recent genocidal event? The summer after *Hotel Rwanda* came out, I was hiking with some friends who'd just returned from serving in Rwanda as missionaries. When we started talking about the movie, one of them said, "What most people don't realize is that Rwanda was the most 'Christianized' nation in Africa when the genocide happened. It was the poster child for missionary success." I didn't believe him, or at least didn't want to believe him.

"Impossible," I said, which led to his firing off some statistics about the percentage of Rwandans who claimed to be Christian and the large number of them attending church on a weekly basis.[3] "Some of the victims were worshiping together with their perpetrators only a few weeks before the genocide broke out," he said glibly.

I was angered by the notion that this horrific crime of historic proportions had happened, not amidst the kind of animism and drumbeat my fundamentalist friends had declared to be the root of all evil, but right in church. The ugly juxtaposition of colonialism, tribalism, an incomplete gospel message, and genocide is yet another story of what happens when the color of justice is lacking on our palettes, and just one more in a string of reasons why so many people don't believe in the God of the Bible.

Stories about the church's complicity with the high crimes of oppression, torture, colonialism, slavery, tribalism, and genocide are plentiful. There are enough of them painting the canvas of history that anyone looking for a good excuse to dismiss the faith outright can, through selective reading, make a case. But they'll need to work hard at *not* listening too, for the truth is that wherever there's ugliness, there's eventually an outbreak of the kind of beauty that can only be described as supernatural. This is where we gain a glimpse into the second primary color: lovingkindness, or, as it's often called, mercy.

REDEFINING RESTORATION

In our culture, people who do wrong things are punished through what we call *retributive justice*. That's why, when we've been wronged, we want to make certain the perpetrator suffers and is punished. But this philosophy of justice has severe limitations, as Dr. Howard Zehr noted:

> Criminal justice tends to be punitive, impersonal, and authoritarian. With its focus on guilt and blame, it discourages responsibility and empathy on the part of offenders. The harm done by the offender is balanced by harm done to the offender. In spite of all this attention to crime, criminal justice basically leaves victims out of the picture, ignoring their needs. Rather than promoting healing, it exacerbates wounds. Retributive justice often assumes that justice and healing are separate—even incompatible, issues.[4]

In contrast, the means of finding justice in ancient Israel was centered on the pursuit of *shalom*, which is always more about the presence of wholeness, with everything made right, than it is about the mere absence of conflict. The reality is that the conflict can be over, and the perpetrators of the crime behind bars, and yet all the people involved might remain entrenched in the wounds of bitterness, shame, isolation, fear, and even lust for vengeance. I've watched people lose sleep, weight, appetite, health, joy, and peace, because they were the victims of some sort of injustice and, even though the perpetrator was punished, they somehow failed to escape the prisons of their own pain and bitterness. The notion of authentic reconciliation is missing in our model.

Somehow, we need to find a way to bring genuine whole-ness to everyone, both perpetrator and victim. This is what has happened in Rwanda. In the wake of horrific genocide, this country is showing us how the colors of *justice* and *mercy* come together to produce one of history's most profound examples of restoration and healing. When the Rwandan government released the perpetrators, they had a clear outcome in mind; their goal was reconciliation, which included the goal of victims forgiving their perpetrators.

This is absolutely vital, because it's through the power of forgiveness, which is a sort of purified form of lovingkindness, that victims are able to shed their load and gain strength to become people of blessing, in spite of their profound losses. As Catherine Claire Larson writes,

> When I see a country known for radical brutality
> becoming, person by person, a place known for radical
> forgiveness, I want to understand. While this process
> is far from complete, every instance is so beautiful, so
> extraordinary, so beyond ordinary human capability, that it
> demands our attention and exploration.[5]

AS WE FORGIVE?

If you're in a church that prays what's come to be known as the Lord's Prayer, then you know these words, drawn from

Jesus' teaching: ". . . and forgive us our debts, as we also have forgiven our debtors."[6] They might roll off our tongue as easily as the Pledge of Allegiance if we've grown up saying them a little too often without thinking.

Maybe we should pay attention to what we're saying. We're asking God to forgive us according to the same standard we're presently forgiving others. The "others" in need of forgiveness, by people praying this prayer on any given Sunday in any given church, will include all forms of perpetrators: sexual predators, spouse abusers, drunk drivers, unfaithful husbands and wives, and shady business partners whose actions leave families destitute. We're not taught to pray, "Forgive me, Lord, because you're so forgiving, and because you did that thing on the cross that somehow enables me to fail over and over again while you continue to treat me like royalty." We're taught to ask God to forgive us in the same way we forgive those who've messed us over. *Do you really want that standard of forgiveness?* Me neither. That's why we'd better change our view of "lovingkindness" and make it a primary color on our palette.

Rwanda shows us the way because after the genocide, by 2003, its prison system was drastically overcrowded, so much so that even with a fully functioning legal system, they were facing a backlog of cases that might have taken at least two hundred years to address. The first step in dealing with this crisis was taken on January 10, 2003, when the president released forty thousand perpetrators.

In America, I know that sometimes people get edgy when an ex-convict moves into a neighborhood. We're suspicious, fearful even. We're not necessarily convinced that there's been a real transformation, even though this person is nothing more to us than a name. The wall between the "ex" and the rest of society is gigantic—and in too many cases it never comes down. Rwanda's "release challenges" are exponentially bigger.

Imagine if you'd grown up with a great neighbor. He and your father were good friends, so much so that he threw you a party the day you were confirmed at church. They've been best friends for twenty years, until the day when tribal hatred causes something to snap inside him. He murders your dad; beats him with a club while others slice into him with machetes. As a daughter, you're hunted too, and flee for your life, and while you're on the run, you learn who killed your dad. Imagine that by the time you could return, your home and property had been destroyed and you'd lost everything to the violence. Now, nine years later, your dad's killer is being released. How would you feel?

Imagine if your husband had been forced to watch as you were raped, and then he was later killed, while another, and then still another man repeatedly raped you as the rest of your entire village either fled or were murdered. Imagine that, in your search for safety, one man offered to bring you food every night while you were in hiding but raped you each time he came. You have AIDS. Your second husband has already died from it. And now the "food for sex" rapist is being released. How would you feel?

Rwandans no doubt had similar feelings. One man had over a hundred family members murdered, and his first response when he heard prisoners were being released was fear, wondering if, once liberated, they would be intent on finishing what they'd begun. That fear is understandable, as are bitterness, hatred, and desire for vengeance.

MERCY TRIUMPHS OVER JUDGMENT

Psalm 85:10 says that "lovingkindness [mercy] and truth have met together." This powerful verse reminds us there will never be any real mercy unless that mercy unfolds in the light of true truth. Jeremiah once complained that the false prophets of his nation healed the wounds of the people "superficially."[7] I've been in situations where there've been fake apologies; everyone in the room knew we'd gone through some motions without anything meaningful being accomplished. As I grow older, I've an increasingly strong distaste for such rubbish, and that's the kindest word I can choose.

For meaningful reconciliation, justice and mercy, truth and lovingkindness must all be present. If I were to paint with too broad a brush, I'd say that conservatives are generally better at the justice/truth side of the equation, and liberals are better at the mercy/lovingkindness side. Both sides are legitimate, but both sides are incomplete without the other, neither justice nor mercy being able, alone, to provide real healing. This is why it's so amazing that Jesus lived here on earth "full of grace and truth."[8] He showed the way for these two seemingly incompatible worldviews to become one. Since both pieces are needed for real reconciliation, the church was called in to help in Rwanda as part of the reconciliation project.

One of the men involved was Gahigi, a pastor who'd lost 142 family members in the genocide. He'd been captured in April of 1994, herded onto a cattle truck with dozens of others, and driven out into an open field to be killed. Gahigi was one of a few who'd managed to slip away into the forest while the slaughter unfolded.

Mattias, a Hutu, was one of the perpetrators, killing with his machete, slicing victims open like fruit. He and the others would form a line, like a search party, and sweep through swamps and forests in search of hiding Tutsis, murdering whomever they found. Two of Gahigi's children died that day, and when he returned to the field that night, the only survivor amid the carnage was his five-year-old son, whose arm had been cut off. The two of them managed to make it across the border to a refugee camp, but his son died there.

When the genocide ended, Gahigi went home, but "home"

had become an entirely different world than what he'd left months earlier. Everything had been taken from him, and he needed to find a way to live in this new void. The default patterns of the heart pushed him toward bitterness and anger, because even though he was a pastor, he had a human heart like the rest of us. The difference for Gahigi was that he wrestled with these emotions, wrestled with this void, wrestled with God for answers. In other words, Gahigi prayed.

His prayers were answered, but as is often the case with prayer, not how he'd have chosen or expected. It became clear to Gahigi that God had a task for him, that he was to go and preach in the prisons, to the perpetrators, about the lovingkindness and mercy of God, his capacity to both forgive and reconcile.

There are lessons to be learned here. Gahigi's capacity to forgive, serve, and become the embodiment of lovingkindness didn't just spring up in him, even though he knew Christ. It didn't come about because he knew the right thing to do, or because light and power fell on him spontaneously from heaven. He needed to wrestle with the reality of his own hatred and work to overcome it. We can't become different people until we face who we are, and in a culture of victimization our victim identity can become so entrenched that we're blinded to our own bitterness and hatred. The moral high ground isn't ever ours automatically. As with mountaineering, we need to do some climbing to get there.

The challenge is that this perspective is so rare, so unearthly, as to be considered unattainable. To continue with the climbing metaphor for a moment, there were centuries when nobody ventured onto summits, believing them to be the habitation of evil spirits. Later, because of the inhospitable environment, humans saw the higher summits as unattainable; the air was too thin or too cold. People would surely die. "Nobody goes there" was conventional wisdom.

It's conventional wisdom still when it comes to the matter of victims expressing mercy and forgiveness to perpetrators. "We're the *victims* here," we say self-righteously. "Why should we need to change?" Our insistence keeps us stuck on lower ground, and this is why the cycle of violence is so hard to break. Miroslav Volf taught about this challenge right when Serbian forces were establishing rape camps in and around his hometown.

> Forgiveness flounders because I exclude the enemy from the community of humans even as I exclude myself from the community of sinners. But no one can be in the presence of the God of the crucified Messiah for long without overcoming this double exclusion—without transposing the enemy from the sphere of monstrous inhumanity into the sphere of shared humanity and herself from the sphere of proud innocence into the sphere of common sinfulness. When one knows that the torturer will not eternally triumph over the victim, one is free to rediscover that person's humanity and imitate God's love for him. And when one knows that God's love is greater than all sin, one is free to see oneself in the light of God's justice and so rediscover one's own sinfulness.[9]

I NEED TO CHANGE MY VIEW OF "THE OTHER"

To use Volf's word, I need to *transpose* the enemy from the sphere of monstrous inhumanity to the sphere of shared humanity. The older brother in the Bible story about the son who wanders off and lives like hell for a few years is helpful here. The younger brother comes to his senses. He sees what a mess he's made of his life. He returns home. The father is able to open his arms and embrace him, but the older brother isn't. He still sees his sibling not as a person but as a category: rebellious.

I've heard this said so many times that I don't listen anymore: "I love the sinner, but I hate the sin." My response is, "If you love the sinner, why can't you be their friend, have them over to share a meal, go skiing with them?" And then I hear, "Well, I love them, but I don't like them." This is a sure sign, in my opinion, that our "love the sinner and hate the sin" line is a code that dismisses us from having real relationships with someone because their label is all we need to know. In fact, their label is the one thing we need to drop, because whoever they are—gay, Muslim, drunk driver, environmentalist, terrorist, genocide perpetrator—they are always, *always*, more than their label, as we've already seen in chapter 2.

By wrestling in prayer, Gahigi was able to come to a point of seeing the other in the sphere of what Volf calls "shared humanity." When we've been victimized by injustice, we stop seeing people and only see the label we've attached to them: thief, cheater, abuser. As long as we remain stuck in that labeling phase, we remain stuck as fellow perpetrators in the ongoing cycle of vengeance and retaliation, even if we never pick up a machete. I need to change my view of the other, losing the label and seeing him/her as part of the human family. There's only one way to do that.

I NEED TO CHANGE MY VIEW OF MYSELF

Sometimes I'm stuck as the victim in what Volf calls "the sphere of proud innocence." My thinking, in my lesser moments, goes something like this: *Bad things have happened to me, and I'll not rest until bad things have happened to the one who did bad things to me. That's the only thing that will bring balance back into the world.*

Gahigi came to see things differently. He saw his own desire for vengeance and retaliation not as understandable, or justifiable, but as sin. This conviction is rooted in the ethic of Christ, who calls us to non-violence, and forgiveness, and loving our enemies. Watching his son die in his arms served to reveal

Gahigi's own heart issues, his own hatred and incapacity to forgive. This is why he prayed and wrestled with God.

And this is how he was transformed. He began visiting prisons with a mission and a message from God. By his fourth visit, after meeting prisoners privately the first few times, Gahigi spoke to a large gathering of perpetrators about getting right, both with God and with the families of those they'd murdered. One man approached him immediately after, weeping and asking for mercy. Gahigi recognized the man, who confessed that he'd both destroyed Gahigi's house and killed his sister.

"I spent many sleepless nights over you. I searched for you so I could kill you," said the man. "But have mercy on me and forgive me." Gahigi embraced the man, who continued to plead for forgiveness. As his sister's murderer bitterly wept in his arms, Gahigi sensed God saying, "This is the purpose for which you are here, and you have seen it with your very own eyes." That day Gahigi embraced not just a killer but what he believed was his calling to be a mediator.[10]

When you read *As We Forgive* or see the movie by the same name[11] (both are worth your time), you'll find an undeniable beauty filling the landscape of Rwanda. It's in the eyes of victims after they wrestle through the dark night of the soul, moving from bitterness to forgiveness. It's in the eyes of the perpetrators after they courageously face their victims and, with humility, confess and ask for forgiveness. It's in the face of Gahigi as he sits with both sides, time after time, case after case, doing the work of rebuilding by cultivating the soil in which reconciliation can grow.

THE BEAUTY OF MERCY

Wherever lovingkindness has become flesh and blood, there's been an outbreak of beauty and healing. In the fall of

2006, Charles Roberts took hostages from a one-room Amish schoolhouse, eventually shooting and killing five girls between the ages of six and thirteen before killing himself. It was only a matter of hours before some from the Amish community were meeting with the members of *his* family, offering them comfort and extending forgiveness. Perhaps the most powerful testimony of the Amish community's capacity for forgiveness happened when several of the victims' parents attended Roberts' funeral, the day after burying their own daughters.

This mercy, this lovingkindness, is deeply rooted in a kingdom "not of this world." In the midst of a world that carries pain and exacts retaliation, the counselors of the reconciliation project in Rwanda have gone to great lengths to teach that Christ has taken *both* the perpetrators' sins and the victims' agony to the cross. He's "borne our griefs" and "carried our sorrows," and it's true: "by His stripes, we are healed."[12]

DOWN OR UP—IT'S OUR MOVE

This kind of beauty is just waiting to be born, and as we've seen, wherever it's born its light is conspicuous. The darkness of revenge and bitterness has the vast majority of the world stuck in a cycle of violence and retaliation, and each act draws us further and further away from our calling as artisans of hope. Our rucksacks get weighed down with immense baggage as we hold on to bitterness over our absent parents, or our divorced parents, or our abusive uncle, or our unfaithful spouse.

All of this stuff is terribly painful, and not to be minimized. But it's stuff that will destroy us unless we learn to let go of it and practice the lost art of lovingkindness. It's a primary color, intended to infuse everything we do, as God reminds us when he tells us to be slow to anger and to avoid bitterness. There are three important ways forward.

First, we need to learn how to practice forgiveness and

lovingkindness in the little things of life. Once, at a Christian seminar, there was a great deal of talk about the dangers of temper and bitterness, how these attitudes could make us physically ill, not to mention the credibility problems we'd create for Jesus as pastors. We all nodded our heads and wrote stuff down. Then when the seminar ended at 4:30, we all rushed to get out of the parking lot at the conference center, so that we could get onto the parking lot that was the freeway.

Another pastor and I saw the same opening in traffic and went for it. He won. I got mad and honked my horn, and he turned around and waved me off. *What a jerk,* I thought. *Didn't he learn anything?* An hour later, still stuck in traffic, I saw my own hypocrisy and failure. If we're going to climb to the top, it will be step by tiny step, and lots of these steps will be made by forgiving people every day in little things, recognizing that we likewise operate in self-interest too often.

Second, we need to drop the labels, because when I label someone, I reduce them from who they are, a person created in God's image, to a one-dimensional creature defined by their crime, or worldview, or sexual orientation, or net worth, or political party. When I do that, I can't love them, and if I can't love them, the art I'm creating through my life will be ugly.

Finally, we need to let go of the big stuff, and this isn't easy.[13] Someone wrote a bitter review of the book *Forgiveness Is a Choice* because they said the title implied they could choose to either keep their bitterness or forgive their unfaithful husband of twenty-six years, and find freedom in either position. Then they came to find out that the premise of the book is that you have freedom to choose to forgive or to choose to be bitter, but that the latter choice will shackle you, affecting your health and all your relationships. The reviewer didn't like that news, and there are times when I don't either, but it's true. Getting there will take some work, but your mountain is no bigger than a Rwandan's, and they've already shown us the way.

INTIMACY

Cosmic Mentoring and Empowerment

Rest in my arms; sleep in my bed; there's a design to what I did and said.[1]

    –SUFJAN STEVENS

We know that One is always and irrevocably for us, even though what flows out of us when we listen to the voice of our hearts gives evidence that we are not always for ourselves.

    –DOUG FRANK

Shortly after moving to Seattle to become a pastor again, I met Kevin, in a climbing gym. He started coming to church, and then we went climbing together. Kevin is taller, younger, funnier, stronger, and a much better climber than I am. I'll never forget the moment when, tied together by rope on the rocks of the high desert, he wouldn't let me stop.

Climbs are rated by difficulty, with a 5.0 being similar to walking up a steep hill. With every .1 addition, things get harder, all the way up to 5.14, which is sort of like climbing the front of your house by clinging to the nails and tiny protrusions from the brick and stucco. I climb comfortably up until about 5.8. I can climb 5.9 with great difficulty. On this day, though, I'm trying, for the first time, to climb in the double decimal digits, at 5.10. Kevin's protecting me by belaying, so that if I fall he'll stop me from plummeting the full fifty feet to the earth.

This is hard for someone of my limited skills, and when I come to the most difficult move, three of my fingers are supporting most of my body weight while my feet flail in search of a place to support them. This agonized hunt continues for several seconds until my fingers have had enough and I let go. "Falling," I shout, and Kevin puts a brake on the rope; after a few feet I come to a stop. I'm hanging, spinning around while new blood delivers recovery energy to my fingers and spent arm. "I'm done, man. Lower!" This is the part where the belayer is supposed to lower you to the ground and congratulate you for a good try.

Instead Kevin says, "I'm not lowering ya, man. You can climb that."

"Funny," I say, acknowledging his attempt at humor. "Lower, please."

"*Not* funny," he says, laughing. "You. Can. Climb. That." He speaks in staccato, punctuating each word to make sure I hear him. I continue to spin, hanging from the rope, about forty-five feet in the air. "Try it again."

Who is this person, telling me what I can and can't do? Friends don't let friends dangle in midair, do they? What did I ever like about him? "No, really. I'm finished."

"No, really. You can climb this." He's not going to let me quit. I need new friends.

I reconnect with the rock, and he tightens the rope as I try again, and fall again. Once more I ask to be lowered. Once more he refuses. Once more I try, and this last time, for reasons still unknown to me, I succeed and finish the climb, exhilarated by the triumph, all the more so because if I'd had my way, we'd already be eating burgers and fries in the middle of nowhere on the way back to Seattle. Kevin saw something in me I didn't and brought it out; he raised my game, so to speak. Good friends do that; so do good coaches. But more than friends or coaches, God does that. God raises our game and brings things out in us that we didn't know were there.

God knows that in order to be the artists we're called to be, we'll need skills we don't have. Acquiring them comes from one thing: *walking with God*. To even have a desire for these skills, we will need the inspiration that comes from walking with God as an example. To develop them, though, we're going to need more than an inspiring example; we'll need a strength of life that comes from walking with God as lover. And finally, to be able to develop the character that cuts utterly against the grain of our desires, we need to learn to walk with God as parent.

WALKING WITH GOD AS EXAMPLE: THE PIANO MAN

And the Word became flesh and dwelt among us, and we saw His glory, glory as of the only begotten from the Father, full of grace and truth.[2]

At the very beginning of his explosive writings, John declares that while Jesus lived here on earth, he did so in a way that made the character of the invisible God visible. Jesus' glory was nothing less than the glory of God.[3] He displayed the perfect interplay of grace and truth, never making the one visible at the other's expense. He served, blessed, healed, confronted, taught, wept, died, and conquered death, all with such perfection that to this very day, millions of people who want nothing to do with organized religion say, "Jesus inspires me to be a better person." Spend time with someone better than you, and you'll discover things about yourself you might want to change.

The Banff Centre is a spectacular retreat facility, located in the heart of the Canadian Rockies. People come from all over the world to study the arts and leadership, and I was fortunate enough to have a friend studying viola there for a year. She invited me north to speak to musicians about the relationship of faith and art. Being a lover of both mountains and music, I thought for about two seconds and then accepted.

My friend was doing a solo with the Calgary Symphony. The rehearsal for this event was preceded by a light supper, attended by most of the symphony members. My friend introduced me to a young woman who couldn't have been five feet tall. She said, "This is Richard, a friend of mine from the States, and he also plays the piano." She shook my hand, and we chatted a bit. I learned that not only was she a student at the Centre, she also was doing a solo piece that night—"the Shostakovich," she said with ease.

We parted ways. I watched the rehearsal. When the short girl sat down at the piano and began to play, the hall exploded with intense, piercing musical beauty. She was not only technically perfect but artistically sensual, drawing even casual listeners into her spell of creative perfection. People gave her a standing ovation *at the rehearsal.*

Afterward, we saw each other, and I thanked her for her profound offering. She said, "I hope I can hear you play before you leave." You have no way of knowing why her comment made me sick to my stomach, so I'll tell you that I was a composition major in college, which meant the piano was a place for me to tinker, which I did on occasion, putting chords together to make pleasant sounds. But if she was a pianistic surgeon, playing with perfect precision, I was a chainsaw. Real music? The discipline of notes? The simplest Bach piece would require weeks of practice to learn, and even then it wouldn't count as real music because I'd slaughter it somehow. Chopin? Forget it.

And *she* wanted to hear *me* play? I told her I'd be pretty busy from right then until the time I left Banff, so "maybe another time," I mumbled, hands in pockets, afraid if she saw them she'd know I was a fraud. After listening to her, I knew I'd been stretching the definition of "I play piano" nearly to the breaking point. I didn't want to touch a piano ever again.

Jesus is the piano man, the prodigy, the genius. He lived well—so well, in fact, that when we take a serious look at how he spent his time, and with whom, we begin to glimpse new heights of both truth-telling and forgiveness, generosity and calls for exacting discipleship, love poured out, and righteous indignation displayed. Walk with him, learn from him, hold your life in the light of his, and you'll see that by comparison, you're likely still a beginner like I am.

Jesus didn't just live the example for us; he spoke of it too. If I were to paraphrase some of his Sermon on the Mount for us and our time, it would sound like this:

> Remember that relationships are more important than religious rituals, so don't hide in church while you're in the midst of contentious relational meltdowns or potential lawsuits. Keep everything as open as possible relationally, because your love for one another is more important than church attendance.[4]
>
> You've heard that it's important to stop sleeping around. But I'm telling you that it's important to stop treating women or men as objects who exist for your sexual pleasure, even if you only play that game in your mind.[5]
>
> Conventional wisdom says that retaliation is the way to respond when wronged. This might be a way to respond, but it's not my way to respond. I'm telling you to love your enemies, and to be generous with them,

recognizing that I've blessed them with the gift of life, just like I've blessed you. So if someone tries to take the shirt off your back, give him your coat too. Pour a little blessing on them in my name. This is how you paint pictures of hope.[6]

By the end, it's as if Jesus has played a concerto of such stunning beauty that our attempts are revealed for what they are, at best the well-meaning efforts of little children. We think that by recycling, joining the ONE campaign (www.one.org), skipping lattes for a month and giving the money to charity, or going to a concert to raise funds for a famine in Africa, we're artisans of hope.

And, of course, in a limited sense that's true.[7] But when we see Jesus' colors, hear his music, we realize that there's more to it than simply giving up a bit from our abundance, or just staying sober. He's calling us to a different level of artistry, a level we can only understand by walking humbly with God.

JESUS AS LOVER: THE SOURCE OF FRUIT IN THE CHRISTIAN LIFE

If Jesus were only an example, we'd eventually come to the discouraging realization that our best attempts to imitate his example will continue to fall miserably short.

That's why it's important to realize that Jesus wants to provide more to us than just an example; he's inviting us into a love relationship, a marriage, and grasping this will make all the difference.

I've been married more than thirty years. One of the things that happened, precisely because we enjoy each other so much, is that we gave birth to three children. Yes, I know it's not really fair to say "we" when talking about giving birth. My wife is the one who needed to carry that life around for such a long time. In our case, she was also the one who needed to fly off the island during labor, adding the bumps of air pockets in flight to the contractions of birthing. In any real way, the pain of delivery was wholly hers.

The life that was born, on the other hand, was wholly a "we" thing. It wouldn't have happened without both of us being involved. It's because we were walking together as husband and wife, man and woman, that we were able to create life.

This is the very thing Jesus is talking about when he tells us to abide in him and that the byproduct of doing so is that we'll "bear much fruit."[8] You could maybe argue that this was some sort of poetic analogy about Jesus being an inspiring example, were it not for Paul developing this line of thought in his letter to the Ephesians:

> "For this reason a man shall leave his father and
> mother and shall be joined to his wife, and the two shall
> become one flesh." This mystery is great; but I am speak-
> ing with reference to Christ and the church.[9]

Paul has been talking about marriage, but here in this passage he's quite clear that marriages work (when they work best) in the same way the relationship between Christ and the church works. In both cases, the wife receives a source of life from her husband, the love of her life. That life is carried in her, united with her, and then born into the world as a unique expression of beauty.

The church is called "the bride of Christ," and as recipients of his life, now present within us through union, we become "pregnant with possibilities," confident that because his life is united with ours, we'll be able to bring forth life. This sounds more mystical than it is. God is telling us that when we "walk with God," receiving his life in a relationship of love and intimacy, we become filled with his life.

The late Major Ian Thomas, founder of the Torchbearers ministry, of which I'm a part, understood this quite well:

> As a young evangelist, my love and enthusiasm for Christ as my Saviour kept me very, very busy until out of sheer frustration, I finally came to the point of quitting. That was the turning point which transformed my Christian life. In my despair I discovered that the Lord Jesus gave Himself FOR me, so that risen from the dead He might give Himself TO me, He who IS the Christian Life.
>
> Instead of pleading for help I began to thank Him for all that He wanted to be, sharing His Life with me every moment of every day. I learned to say "Lord Jesus, I can't, You never said I could; but You can, and always said You would. That is all I need to know." From that moment life became the adventure that God always intended it to be.[10]

Let's pause here. The author of the letter to the Hebrews asked his readers to fix their "eyes on Jesus, the author and perfecter of faith."[11] Most of us get the "author" part; Jesus came, lived an exemplary life, and died on our behalf.[12] But the "perfecter" piece is simply vital to experiencing the reality of transformation, because without it, we're forgiven by the death of Christ but left to somehow perfect ourselves. The seminar circuit and amazon.com's self-help section tell us two things: (1) People are trying to transform themselves, and (2) it's not working very well.

The better way is to live, day by day, in the experience of union with Christ, utterly assured, by faith, that we're filled with his life.[13] This fullness enables us to be fruitful, giving birth to a beauty that is a unique expression of Christ's life united with our own. Sure, someone may have had medical talent anyway, but that talent united with Christ means the doctor

retires early in order to work in refugee camps wherever terror and natural disasters strike. Our union with Jesus doesn't
mean we're no longer recognizable any more than we lose our
identity when we get married. But in both cases, union means
creation of something new, something hopeful, redemptive,
through our life together.

We need more than an example; we need a lover to fill us
with divine life!

JESUS AS PARENT

When I was first married, my wife and I discovered a buffet place up by the Canadian border that had seafood Fridays.
I don't know how they did it, but they offered king crab legs,
oysters, salmon, and several other fish dishes as part of their
all-you-can-eat supper for about eight bucks.

I'd skip lunch and sometimes even breakfast on buffet days.
All day long I'd think about the great event that was coming
later, when our family would walk through the doors of King's
Table and I'd eat the foods I loved until eating was no longer
possible.

My wife's plate was always balanced: a nice salad, with
some string beans and broccoli. Not me. I was a vegetarian's
worst nightmare, loading my plate with things that had been
killed rather than picked. She'd look at me and roll her eyes.
"No broccoli?" she'd ask. I'd smile, glad I was an adult, able to
make my own bad decisions.

I had, of course, managed to convince myself I was eating
healthily, telling myself that because I did a few pushups once
in a while, I was in strength training, which meant I needed lots
of protein. Ha. What I needed was antioxidants and micronu-
trients, the kind found in green things. What I needed was to
learn to eat things I didn't like.

And therein is the challenge. Why, if it's a buffet line, would you subject yourself to wasting precious space in your stomach on food you don't like, denying yourself the pleasure of eating only your favorites? It's those favorites that excite us and give us pleasure, and because of this we'll pick them every time.

We're not just talking about food, either. When it comes to how we build our lives, the reality is that many of us in the prosperous West face a virtual buffet of economical, vocational, geographical, political, and educational choices. Shall I live in the Northwest, or the Southeast? Should I travel after college or go to graduate school? Should I marry him? Date her? Buy that? We're building our lives like we build a plate full of food; we survey the options and choose what's best for us, what we call "our passion."

Let's not dismiss the value of finding your passion. It can lead to amazing things. The problem, though, is that when we build our lives by serving up portions from the buffet table of options, we surely run the risk of skipping our equivalent of broccoli while we load up on our existential version of king crab legs and salmon, all because of a focus on finding our passion. So here we are, building a customized life in every way: economically, financially, geographically, vocationally, educationally. It's in line with passion. But it's not balanced, or healthy.

Meanwhile, what if God's over there in the corner, trying to get our attention because he's got something green for our plate (or maybe, if you're vegan, he's got some steak and eggs!). What will we do about that? Will we receive the broccoli? Will we eat the collard greens and kale? Adding these things to our plate, of course, will have the effect of forcing us to take some other things off as well. We'll need to let go of some plans we have, and some of those plans might be things about which we're passionate.

The fact is, God is like a good parent. There are things he

wants to put on our plate that we wouldn't choose. Jeremiah didn't want to be a prophet. It wasn't his passion. When God first spoke to him about the job, he told God as much, told God he was too young. Later, after his ministry resulted in rejection, and suffering, and plots against his life, he complained about his calling. Ultimately, though, he decided it's better to suffer in the will of God than pursue happiness on individual terms. Jeremiah ate his greens.

So did Paul. He had a passion to serve among Jewish people and told God so. But God's response was to give him a better idea: Paul's destiny was to serve among the Gentiles. Broccoli. The same thing was true for Peter; Jesus said it was in his destiny to go some places he would never choose to go, do some things he wouldn't want to do.

There's some broccoli in my story as well. I went to seminary with the intention of becoming a teacher and toward the end of my studies had flown to Alaska to interview with a small Bible college, where I'd teach a little bit of music and a lot of Bible classes. Everything was set, except that the job wouldn't begin for nearly a year. It was while we were waiting to move to Alaska that a church on a small island in the Pacific Northwest called me on the phone and invited me to visit because they needed an interim pastor for a few months while they searched for a permanent one. The island is accessible only by ferry or plane. I thought, *What harm could there be in flying up there and checking this out?*

A family on the east side of this tiny island put me up for the weekend in their cabin, a little house down on the water. I'd arrived in the dark, so nothing could have prepared me for the next morning. I woke up and looked out the window eastward, where an overwhelming beauty assaulted my eyes. The sky was painted with color, framing the silhouette of a mountain bathed in glacial ice, even then, in August. The rest of the Cascade

Mountains played supporting roles, and as the sun came up shafts of light pierced the water that stood between the mainland and the forested island. The whole setting was too much, literally taking my breath away. That I'd lived in the concrete forests of Los Angeles for the past three years perhaps made the scenery even more stunning, similar to how food tastes more intense after fasting.

I preached, spoke with people about my plans to teach, and learned about this small church on this small island that was looking for someone to care for them until the permanent pastor came along. I called my wife back in Los Angeles, where it was 104° and smoggy. I was wearing a sweater, inhaling pristine, cool air, and looking out the window as the glacial ice on the mountain to the east turned pink during sunset. "Is it pretty there?" she asked. "Sort of," I said, afraid that if I told her how heavenly it really was, all our decision-making objectivity would fly out the window.

And that was that. I went home and we moved a thousand miles north within a month. It didn't matter in the least to me that being a pastor wasn't my passion. It was only temporary. I won't go into all the details of how it happened, but the "interim" became six years involving a growing church, a new building, lots of weddings, some funerals, walking with people through the valleys of disappointment and loss, and many challenges. That was over two decades ago. Somewhere along the way, I became something I neither sought nor expected to be: a pastor.

I generally loved my years on the island and thoroughly enjoyed the friendships formed there. But on more than a few days I wrestled with God about my calling because the reality was that I didn't like the title "pastor." I'd cringe when people said, "Hello, Pastor Dahlstrom," and even got to the point of responding, "Well, hello, Civil Engineer Dave," as a not so subtle way of saying, "Why do you call me by my title?" You see, I'd become a pastor at a time in American history when the image of "pastor" was associated more with greed, arrogance, hypocrisy, and sexual scandal than with someone who helps people walk with God and helps shapes communities to become people of hope.

Being a pastor is messy work because you're dealing with real things like divorce, job loss, drug addictions, and people dying of cancer when they're only twenty-two. People call you when life isn't working out well. Sometimes, when people are making destructive choices, it falls on the pastor to call on them and say things they don't want to hear. This leads to conflict, and I spent most of my growing-up years avoiding the messiness of conflict, preferring the peace of superficiality to the liberating but sometimes painful intensity of truth.

I wanted none of this. I wanted what I naïvely thought would be the sanitized world of a little Bible college in the north country, where I could go snowmobiling with young and relatively innocent college students, imparting whatever wisdom I could to them before they went out into the real world. Church work? Pastoring? Way too messy for my choosing, the broccoli of my vocational world.

It turns out, though, God has continued to heap this broccoli on my plate down through the years. I moved off the island to the mountains to start a study center and ended up starting a church there too. Then I moved to Seattle because a church there thought I should consider being the pastor of their flock. I didn't think so but did the interviews anyway and in the end it was perfectly clear I was to move to Seattle. Our family ended up leaving a ministry in the mountains that we loved in order for me to become a full-time pastor again.

The most vibrant hope requires an emptying of ourselves, which means an emptying of our agendas, biases, ambitions, and yes, even our own life. It's this emptying that enables us to demonstrate a kind of otherworldly love. Jesus said it was this particular love that would bring life to the world.[14] Then, most dramatic and challenging of all, he said this love's clearest demonstration comes from laying down one's life for another.

Of course, he did just that, going to the cross at the expense of his own desires and agenda. This is a large part of what it means to "walk with God," for the truth is we're called to walk with Jesus by sharing in his self-emptying and suffering so that we can share in his glory and resurrection life as well. We can't pick and choose those parts we'll share with him, because Jesus isn't a buffet line. The colors of self-denial and the cross belong to us, and when they're mixed together, they create vibrant colors of hope on the canvas of our world.

Jesus' followers have been painting this same picture in unique ways all across the pages of history. Sometimes their expressions have been dramatic, like Peter being crucified upside down as a martyr, or Dietrich Bonhoeffer returning to Germany as the Third Reich was on the rise, knowing that he was doing so at risk to his life. Other times, the same spirit of laying down one's life has been more subtle, but perhaps nonetheless difficult, as in the case of the folks who loved and prayed for the man who killed the children in the schoolhouse, or the couple who sold everything and invested their retirement in building clinics in Africa.

These are the clearest, truest colors of hope. They're clear because, just as Jesus burst forth from the grave with all the vibrancy of resurrection life, the best colors of hope can only be born on the far side of self-denial. The truth of the matter is that if life is a buffet line, I'll not choose to put self-denial on my plate. Once again, for those who follow Jesus, life isn't a buffet line. Jesus knows our passions, and our desires, and he's a good shepherd, often blessing us with the gift of being able to do things we love.

He also knows us better than we know ourselves and, because of this, knows where we'll need to say no to our own desires in order to say yes to birthing the kind of vibrant hope that only resides on the far side of the cross. Jesus knows all about this, because he went there first. What we find often is that after our wrestling, and resisting, and then finally saying yes to God, this element of self-denial has taken us into contexts and callings where we can only marvel as we say, "I was born for this." To return to the beginning of the chapter, God knows when to let us rest and when to push us; when to encourage and when to correct. He knows how to raise us up to attain our true destiny.

I want to be an artist capable of imparting beauty and hope to this broken world, but there have been more than a few times I've been so busy creating on my own that I've lost touch with the One whose vision for wholeness I'm supposed to be embodying in my life and words, and works. I've been autonomous, creating out from my own interests and passions, drifting slowly but inexorably into the independence that I deeply crave. But eventually I find that the stuff I do on my own is both exhausting and unsatisfying.

Being a pastor was the food the Shepherd put on my plate twenty-five years ago. I can't tell you how grateful I am that, in spite of so much within me that resisted, I was able to eat my greens. Why? Because after all these years, I can now say with joy, "I was born for this." And because I know there are still more new menu items the Shepherd has for me, I'll keep walking with God, I pray, until the very end.

8

PASTEL FANTASY

God's Use of Deep Colors

*Any given moment confronts us with a given reality. If it is
a given, it is a gift. If it is a gift, the appropriate response is
thanksgiving. Yet thanksgiving, where it is genuine, does not pri-
marily look at the gift and express appreciation; it looks at the
giver and expresses trust.*

—David Steindl-Rast

*Shall we indeed accept good from God and not accept
adversity?*[1]

—Job

PRECIOUS MOMENTS IN PASTEL

There's a danger right at this point in our consideration of
God's primary colors. The primary colors of justice, mercy,
and walking humbly with God can create, if we're not careful, a
romantic notion of our calling to spill hope. We might come to
believe that the process of spilling these colors into the world,

because it is the right way to live, will be easy, or at the very least, pleasant. We'll be, as Jesus calls us to be, shining as lights in this darkened world, and this will mean that the moths of the world will be drawn to us or to our endeavors, resulting in new colors and beautiful pictures on the canvases of lives, institutions, and cultures touched by our efforts carried out in Jesus' name.

All of that might be true sometimes, but to think that this is simply the way it works because we have a vision for God's reign demonstrates the kind of naïveté that often becomes rich soil for disillusionment and defection from God's good work. What's needed is not a romantic notion of how things will work out, but a realistic one. Maybe an analogy will help.

I remember, as a small child, seeing a funny Bible (my older sister's) with pastel pictures of the most famous Bible scenes in it. Everyone is wearing pastel colors: purple, mauve, or girlish pink, with maybe a splash of weak yellow thrown in for effect. And of course, everyone's also wearing a serenity smile, the kind you have when you've finished a good meal. You know the scenes: Noah's inviting happy animals into the ark. David is strumming on his harp while contented sheep listen serenely at his feet. The angel visits Mary, delivering the good news of her impending motherhood. And then, of course, there's Jesus. He's breaking loaves and feeding thousands, raising a little girl from the dead and teaching eager listeners, also dressed in pastels, just like the main stars. Eventually he will rise from the dead with a nice pastel robe hiding the icky scars that mar his hands and feet.

It was in this precious world that I learned about the God who loves creation, loves humanity, freely sharing many good things with his children, the greatest gift of all being Jesus himself, who demonstrates his love by blessing people through his life, death, and triumph over the grave in a marvelous pastel resurrection scene.

This Bible, carried in hand by both my older sister and many of her friends, had the same text as any other Bible. All the stories were there. But of course, what gets the pastel brush and what doesn't has the effect of sending a message about who God is, what God values, and how the life of faith is to be lived. And the message of the pastel Bible seemed to be that a deep sense of contentment and satisfaction is the birthright of every follower of Jesus. God is in the business of orchestrating our lives in such a way that good things happen to those who know and love him.

My experiences at church camp reinforced the pastel worldview. Every year at camp, around Thursday night, all of us twelve-, thirteen-, or fourteen-year-olds would be sitting out under the stars, encircling a roaring campfire. Our week had been filled with foot races, swimming holes, picnics, skits, crafts, singing, and Bible talks, all of which pointed us to Thursday, when campfire time would be filled with testimonials. What had we learned? How had our lives changed? And most significantly, what were we going to leave up in the high country when we went "down the mountain," back to the valley where real life must be lived? People would share what had happened over the course of the week and throw stuff in the fire that was holding them back in their faith journey, stuff like booze, bad magazines, and tobacco.

I loved Thursday night campfire because it was inevitable that all of us would shed some tears, shed some sin, hug our friends and counselors, and cement some sort of decision in our hearts that we would, with the best of intent, attempt to take back down the mountain. It was a major pastel moment, bathed in a holy campfire glow.

And this was the Christian life for me. I was, as a child, in pursuit of an endless string of these pastel moments. After all, they're the moments that get illustrated in my sister's Bible;

they're the moments that comprise the core narratives of all Sunday school curricula up until at least seventh or eighth grade. They're the point, really. Love, joy, peace, patience, kindness, goodness—these are the soft colors of the faith life, and basking in the emotions and experiences associated with them is the goal.

Some of us were able to pull it off, at least for a while. I grew up in a home where Mom and Dad loved each other. Dad worked. Mom stayed home, and this meant there were chocolate chip cookies, fresh from the oven, waiting for us when we got home. She volunteered in various church activities, especially investing her time in caring for people who couldn't care for themselves. Usually, she was home from whatever it was she was doing in time to have some nice hot food on the table for us, so that we could eat as a family of four, giving thanks and then listening as either Mom or Dad read a devotional. We watched *Lassie* and *I Love Lucy*. Dad and I mowed the chemically fortified lawn on Saturdays and finished just as Mom's spaghetti sauce was bubbling on the stove, the smells of pasta, salami, and tomatoes wafting through the house. Saturday nights were games or more television, and Sunday morning was a full time at church.

A rhythm developed in that childhood which, looking back, was very pleasant, content—pastel even. I grew up in that window of peace after the Korean War, and was still very young when the disillusionment of Vietnam was in full bloom. While we did have nuclear attack drills because of the Cold War (which consisted, hysterically, of hiding under our desks!), life was quite a bit like *Leave It to Beaver*, where the really big crises had to do with spilling things at the supper table or losing a Little League game.

Our lives were very pastel because, like the illustrators of that Bible, our parents went to great lengths to highlight those colors and shield us from the less pleasant ones. I was well into my teens before realizing that the reason my sister and I were adopted was because our adoptive mother lost her first child at birth, nearly resulting in her own death, and precluding her from having children. Nor did I know, until about that same time, that my adoptive dad had been in and out of the hospital numerous times with pneumonia as a child, and again during the war, severely compromising his lungs and thus restricting his activities. This would eventually lead him to an early grave at the age of fifty-three.

When that happened, I was only seventeen. Dad's death had the effect of spilling deep red blood across the canvas of my carefully controlled and constructed pastel world. It wasn't pretty. That same year, a friend one year younger than me died when a drunk driver ran a red light at full speed. My friend was a Christian just like me. His world, as much as mine, was filled with beautiful pastel colors, but those colors seemed to offer little protection against the ravages of those who drive after drinking too much. I knew of people in my hometown who were shipped off to Vietnam and failed to make it back.

These setbacks, these blotches, were the basis for my eventual questioning of the faith and my quasi-disengagement from it all. The spilled blood of soldiers, the black marks of Dad's death, and the countless hints at disillusionment and hypocrisies, in the church, political halls, and my own heart, conspired to create a dark grey cloud of depression, which hung over me, muting all the colors on my canvas. Throw in an awakening of my sexuality (something about which I'd heard very little in church) and my own loneliness as I headed away to college and sought to make my mark in the world, and the canvas that was once filled with nothing but a string of precious moments had suddenly become more like some sort of cubist rendition of suffering and angst. I wondered if my faith would survive the collision between the real world I was experiencing and the pastel world I'd learned about in Sunday school.

My own journey back into the vibrancy of faith came from revisiting the Scriptures in the wake of all these tragedies. Instead of finding an endless string of pastel moments, my adult reading of the Bible revealed a full spectrum of colors and experiences. Yes, Joseph hugged his estranged brothers after years of separation in a beautiful pastel reunion. But he was also beaten, tossed in a well, sold as a slave, framed for sexual assault in a foreign land, and imprisoned without a trial. Not very pastel of him, was it? David? In addition to the harp, there's adultery, murder, a coup from within his own family, and the untimely death of his sons. Jesus? Let's not forget about the whip, or his exasperation with the disciples, or his sweating drops of blood in the garden. I could go on, but you get the point.

The life of faith, it seems, is a real life after all. It's a life able to embrace all the colors. There's room for the full range of emotions and experiences. The author of the letter to the Hebrews[2] explains this marvelously: Some people of faith saw resurrections; others were crucified. Some shut the mouths of lions; others happened to be inside those mouths when they were shut. Some were healed miraculously. Others died early. Some saw spectacular deliverance; others were killed by drunk drivers or war bullets. In short, all the colors are there: glory and shame, life and death, success and failure, fidelity and betrayal. But many of us won't believe it until our pastel world collapses.

When Amy Carmichael followed God's call on her life and moved to India, she became involved in the rewarding yet untidy work of helping young women escape temple prostitution. As she developed a family of young women, the work began growing in complexity and scope beyond anything she could have expected. Why, then, did she step into a hole while examining a construction project, permanently injuring her back in the process so that she was bedridden the rest of her days?

My sister (the one with the pastel Bible) had just finished singing at a Thanksgiving concert on a Thursday night. She had the voice of an angel, and the countenance to match. Her personality was so endearing that everyone she knew thought they were her best friend. An artist, craftswoman, mother to four young children, and gifted musician, all her talents were used in the service of the Jesus she loved. Her home was hospitality central and oozed the beauty and warmth of Christ. Why, then, would she wake up the morning after her concert, clutching her chest before passing out and dying of a massive heart attack in her early forties? How does this fit into God's wonderful plans?

I know people who missed Flight 93 out of Boston and were thus spared their deaths on September 11, 2001. We like to tell those stories as Christians, as evidence of "God's faithfulness." But what about the ones who arrived at the airport just in time to catch their flight that morning? Did God take a coffee break at that moment? He could have orchestrated some sort of traffic jam, couldn't he?

GOD'S COLORS

We've seen the pastels and we've seen the blood spilled across the canvas. What do we make of it all? Down through the years, the church has offered several different options for coping with these realities.

Plenty of people would argue we can avoid nasty spills entirely. They'll tell us that health and wealth belong to those who love God and have enough faith to claim the promises and gifts he wants to give us. Thus are we invited to thank God for health, even when we're sick, and for forthcoming wealth, even when we're poverty stricken. There's a sense in which we're invited to "claim" that which, we're told, is rightfully ours. Such faith on our parts will result in God's responsiveness and sickness will flee, even as wealth comes our way.

Such notions aren't fabricated out of thin air. In Deuteronomy 28, God promises Israel health and prosperity in exchange for obedience:

> If you diligently obey the LORD your God, being careful to do all His commandments which I command you today, the LORD your God will set you high above all the nations of the earth. All these blessings will come upon you and overtake you if you obey the LORD your God: Blessed shall you be in the city, and blessed shall you be in the country. Blessed shall be the offspring of your body and the produce of your ground and the offspring of your beasts, the increase of your herd and the young of your flock. Blessed shall be your basket and your kneading bowl. Blessed shall you be when you come in, and blessed shall you be when you go out.[3]

This goes on for another lengthy paragraph, promising victory in battle, a fertile womb, and material and physical blessings at every turn. Of course, this is an enormously attractive notion. Our life becomes a transaction whereby we insert obedience and God delivers blessing. It's easy in such a model to come to the conclusion that any trial, any poverty, any health crisis or setback is directly tied to some moral failing on our part. That's why Jesus' disciples, when they saw a man who'd been born blind, asked Jesus who sinned, the blind man or his parents, that such a thing would happen. Their thinking, in keeping with the Deuteronomy principle, was that there surely must be a moral failing somewhere, someone on whom they could pin the blame, some sin that had resulted in this tragedy. But Jesus says no. It happened for other reasons.

We'd like to believe that the world works neatly, with a tight causal structure so that good things happen to good people, and bad things happen to bad people. That way we can judge the homeless person as lazy, and the sick person as careless with their body, and the person who loses their home as financially reckless. We'd like to think justice is that easy to understand, that God's word to the Jews in the desert back when Moses was about to die is the word for today too: faith + obedience = health and wealth.

This is what makes false promises of health and prosperity in exchange for following Jesus so popular. It's an appealing message because it's natural to desire a life with as little want, deprivation, and suffering as possible. At some level this is appropriate, especially when considered in contrast to the dark pessimism that hangs over some other alternatives, as we'll see in a moment.

God told Israel that their obedience would be rewarded with prosperity, and their disobedience punished with plagues and the loss of health and wealth. There's something incredibly appealing about this kind of contract with God. It's clear; it's swift; it's causal, so that if bad things happen, you know it's because you've been bad. It's also not the way things work anymore.

The cause-and-effect deal handed to Moses was part of a contract between God and Israel. Though the Bible is clear that God doesn't change, the Bible is also clear in declaring that God's ways of revealing himself in the world change, as well as his ways of dealing with his followers. Even by the time of the prophets, this causal link between faithfulness and material blessing was gone. Jeremiah was faithful to God, but his ministry would be counted a resounding failure by any contemporary measures. He was locked in stocks, tossed in a pit, mocked, and beaten (and these at the hands of his "friends"!). John the

Baptist? Beheaded. Peter? Crucified upside down. Paul? "Three times I was beaten with rods, once I was stoned, three times I was shipwrecked, a night and a day I have spent in the deep . . . sleepless nights, in hunger and thirst, often without food, in cold and exposure."[4]

Apparently the deeper colors of pain and deprivation can spill onto the canvas of the faithful as easily as the colors of peace and contentment. Until we wrap our minds and hearts around this, we're in danger of forever seeking to create and live in a pastel world, when what we really need is to learn how to be people of hope in the midst of the bloody colors of suffering, shortcomings, and loss that come with living in a fallen world. Helmut Thielicke, the great German theologian, said that America's inadequate theology of suffering is her Achilles heel, the weakness that, if not addressed, is in danger of rendering her infertile.

Until we stop claiming the Old Testament promises of prosperity and perfect health as our own, we will be forever searching for the right combination of faith and obedience to usher us into Christian nirvana. Sadly, such a search is very self-absorbed, and our calling to love our neighbors and enemies fades into the distance as we dash off to another seminar in search of healing.

SAFETY FIRST

Some are quick to acknowledge that, indeed, bad things do happen to good people, but only because good people are careless. The key to living well is living safely. Lock your doors at night. Get an alarm system. Save 10 percent and make sure your investment is insured. Speaking of insurance, get lots of it for health, life, home, and liability because God knows there are crazy people out there who will take you for all you're worth if you're not careful. Take your vitamins, minerals, omega-3s, ginkgo biloba, and St. John's Wort. Eat lots of soluble fiber. Exercise. Get eight hours of sleep. Tithe. Go to church regularly, being certain to drive carefully both on the way there and on the way home (it's best if your car's the biggest, because then you're the safest). Don't go on mission trips to places where you might contract staph infection, malaria, intestinal parasites, or face a terrorist plot. Risky hobbies? Forget it. Read books instead, or maybe take up pottery or oil painting (but only in a well-ventilated room, because those fumes . . . well, you know.) Eat organic. Get a colonoscopy.

There, that should do it. Now you're safe, right? Well, not really. Pistol Pete Maravich, extraordinary basketball talent and specimen of fine health, died at the age of forty, while shooting hoops. He didn't smoke or drink. Meanwhile, the oldest woman on record, Jeanne Calment, who died at the age of 122, stopped smoking at 117 because her eyesight was so bad she could no longer see clearly enough to light her cigarettes.

The safety-first posture toward living is, when reduced to its basest form, a fear-based posture of living. It's an attitude that says, "If you do everything right, everything in your power to protect yourself from bad things happening, you should make it through just fine." Sadly, though, there's a tradeoff that happens with this. While I may be in pursuit of safety, and while I may greatly increase my chances of achieving it, I do so at some cost to my peace of mind because, like my prosperity friends, I believe that ultimately I'm in control. My wise choices are of enormous importance in assuring my survival and comfort, both of which are extremely important.

This is wrong at several levels. First, and most significantly, the good life is never defined by Jesus in terms of either length or comfort. To the contrary, Jesus says that those who seek to save their life will lose it, and those who lose their lives, spilling them out generously in service to others because of love for God and humanity, will find them. I need to rid myself of the notion that living to be 110 and still able to walk three miles a day is the pinnacle of "the good life." The pages of history are filled with people like Sophie Scholl who died in their twenties because of a commitment to truth, justice, and service.[5] Nobody could ever accuse such saints of having lived anything but the fullest of lives, because fullness isn't defined by Jesus in terms of length but in terms of depth.

The other issue that arises among the safety-first crowd is that this obsession with living carefully has the unintended effect of creating perpetual anxiety. When I'm walking around in a room and then the power goes out, I suddenly become extremely careful with my steps, precisely because I don't know where the sharp edges and corners of the room are, and I want to avoid a trip to the emergency room. This is fine in a darkened room for a few minutes until one finds a candle, but it's possible to live one's entire life with that same anxiety level, always wondering what's coming next, and taking great care to assure ourselves that what's coming next won't hurt us.

This leads to my final observation: While it's fine and even appropriate to do things that will increase our odds of being healthy and keeping our resources, any notions that we're in control of our destiny are pure illusion. I know a person who ate organic foods, exercised, meditated, and took her daily vitamins. She died of cancer in her early fifties. Control? We simply don't have it.

When I counsel couples about to get married, I give them a test; one of the scores that comes back reveals their anxiety. When someone has an exceptionally high level, I'll usually ask them some questions to determine what they're anxious about. Once they've shared their answers (which usually have to do with the wedding, or finances, or some relational stalemate with future in-laws), I'll say, "Is that all? There's so much more you could be anxious about!" They'll look concerned, and then I'll sometimes (depending on many factors related to the couple's emotional health) continue with something like this:

"There's always the possibility of infertility, or an unanticipated pregnancy, and once those children come, what a wild card they can be! Don't forget about the economic uncertainties that come with these days, not to mention the physical and emotional health of your spouse, and I just read on a prophecy website that the dollar is about to go into a freefall because of the obscene national debt, and terrorists might be planning another attack, and . . ." I go on like this for a bit as they sink into their chairs and their eyes get blurry. Then, while the gravity of it all is still sinking in, I finally say, "Are you getting my point? Listen carefully: *Control is an illusion.*"

This usually provides a great segue to a discussion about how, in an uncertain world, Christ offers himself to us as the "anchor of the soul,"[6] and how this Shepherd King walks with us through all of life, both on the heights of triumph and through the valley of the shadow of death. Thus we come to see that we're promised not immunity from suffering, but a great presence, a companion, in the midst of suffering.

CHRISTIANITY NOIR

At the other end of the spectrum from our prosperity and safety friends are those who've had enough of Christian radio, Christian TV, and superficial Christian answers to life's deepest and most perplexing problems. When they encounter people who quote the Bible a lot, or have Christian music on their iPods, they smile condescendingly, as if to say, "Someday you'll get it."

Whether it's been their own, or in the lives of others, it seems that suffering and loss have come to define this subset of people. The landscape of their lives has been filled with enough storms, deprivation, and disillusionment that they've become convinced this is the norm. Like Wesley said in *The Princess Bride*, "Life *is* pain. Anyone who tells you otherwise is selling something."

Such people are rightly skeptical of health, wealth, and prosperity people. They've often seen enough as well to make them doubtful of the safety-first mantra. But this leaves them in a rather barren land, a land where any notions of hope, beauty, peace, and contentment seem like wishful fairy tales. The default position is suffering and loss, and though there may be moments of exception, we'll always return there. These folks love Job but aren't quite sure what to do with Paul's words about rejoicing always. They love the raw honesty of John the Baptist when he had doubts about the identity of Jesus, but they're troubled by the notion that anyone would sing hymns after being beaten and tossed into prison.

The end result of such a perspective is that the cup is invariably half empty, and those who believe otherwise are simply naïve. Once they've tasted reality, the optimists will come to their senses and stop quoting Bible verses, stop singing hymns, stop clinging to medieval notions that "All is well, and all shall be well, and all manner of things shall be well."[7] Hearing from hopeful people, they smile condescendingly and walk away. But their disengagement from hope can become synonymous with a disengagement from calling. "Institutional Christianity is too superficial," they say, as they settle in to a life of eating and drinking with friends, and watching indie films.

In every case we've seen, though the assessment differs as to which colors constitute real faith, the bottom-line problem is the same: *"It's all about me."* It's either about my pain, or my safety, or my faith, or my prosperity, or my health, or my suffering and loss.

Here's an important newsflash: It's not about you. Get over it.

REAL-WORLD FAITH: A FULL PALETTE

Real-world faith defies formulas. As we've already seen, some good people die young, others die old. Some bad people grow wealthy. Others lose everything. Disease strikes the careful and the careless, and seems also to bypass some careless and a few more careful. So what are we to do?

We're to learn how to walk humbly with God, which means learning how to live fully in the midst of both pain and comfort, joy and sorrow, peace and turmoil, prosperity and adversity, and yes, even certainty and doubt. A quick survey of the Bible shows us that those who lived most fully went through the fullest range of experiences and engaged in those experiences honestly with God. It's not all worship and singing, but it's not all tears and doubt. It's not all comfort and family, but it's not all loss and suffering either.

Our capacity to live honestly, fully present across the entire spectrum of experience, is what real-world faith is all about. As we wander through the biographies of those who lived in this full range, we'll come to discover that *it* is normal, that there's "a time for everything" as both the Preacher in Ecclesiastes[8] and the Byrd brothers remind us.

This juxtaposition of joy and sorrow has been my lot. When

my son was born, I spent the night with my wife at the hospital and then rose early the next morning to walk through the small town where the hospital was. It was early in June, and the sun was already up when I walked down to the water, grateful for the birth of a healthy child, amazed that I was now the father of two, and profoundly proud of my wife, who seemed to do this with increasing ease (though perhaps only a male would ever use *ease* and *childbirth* in the same sentence). I sat on a bench, flooded with these emotions, and suddenly began to cry, to weep deeply, because I missed my dad. I wanted him to see me now, wanted him to help me know how to raise a son, wanted to watch him hold out his thumb to my son, the way he'd done with me.

This juxtaposition is life. We're not called to careful or safe living. We're certainly not called to preemptive pessimistic disengagement. The colors of hope will be spilled into the world by broken people, living their broken lives in the midst of a broken world. But right there, in the midst of all the pain and suffering, those who have taken up the adventure of spilling hope will find colors of beauty, justice, healing, and joy being poured through them onto the canvas of their families, churches, and cities. This is the life to which we're called, the adventure that awaits us as broken, yet deeply loved, artisans of hope.

DOING ART WHILE DOING LIFE

Life happens. Job changes, relationship realities, children, parents, sickness, leaky faucets, earthquakes and floods, church meetings, weeds in the garden, shopping, dealing with money, investments turning to ashes. These things are enough to make your head spin all by themselves, never mind the art or the calling to be a blessing.

There's risk that these real and immediate issues will utterly consume us, and if they do, we'll wake up toward the end of our lives and wonder what we did with all our days. If we're going to make movies or cookies, climb mountains or build clinics, teach children or hand out hot chocolate and blankets on the street, we're going to need to make space for it in our lives, and this won't happen accidentally.

PART THREE

CREATING ART WHILE LIFE HAPPENS

These final chapters are about discovering the unique artistry to which each of us is called. Finding this calling is only the first step, though, because knowing what we're created to do doesn't by any stretch mean it will happen. Shame and failure can derail us in an instant, and it happens all the time. Doing battle with these ugly giants is the point of chapter 10.

Chapter 11 is a reminder that other setbacks have less to do with the state of our soul than the state of things in general. Fires, windstorms, economic hardships, organizational challenges—*stuff* happens, and when it does, we'd better learn to read the tea leaves, so to speak, so we know when to walk away and when to dig in our heels and persevere.

Then there's the reality that we're trying to live as people of blessing in the midst of ongoing oceans of change. We simply can't find a formula for living and stick with it, because what works for single people doesn't work anymore when we are married. A healthy twenty-year-old approaches everything differently from someone in their eighties dying of cancer. Navigating the waters of change is addressed in chapter 12.

Most of life is filled with wholly unspectacular moments, and the last chapter exposes how important these moments really are. The reality is that each moment of our lives, each brushstroke of blessing, is a seed sown, and we usually don't know what the fruit of those brushstrokes will be. As I've climbed high up and looked down on the landscape of my life,

I've discovered that countless people were dropping seeds of hope, beauty, affirmation, and encouragement into the soil of my life. Those people have not only shaped me by their blessings, they've become role models, showing me that sowing the seeds of hope, day in and day out, publicly and unheralded, in big ways and small, is how artisans of hope manage to live so well for so long.

9

THE ARTIST'S IDENTITY
Finding Your Voice

*If you really belong to the work that has been entrusted to you,
then you must do it with your whole heart. What you are doing,
I cannot do, and what I am doing, you cannot do. Only sometimes we forget and we spend more time looking at somebody
else and wishing we were doing something else.*

—Mother Teresa

Our refrigerator broke a few years ago. Nearly every attempt I've
ever made to fix something mechanical has resulted in further
damage to already broken items. So when the cooling machine was
whining, I did the smart thing: I stepped away from the appliance
and called around to find someone to fix it. Soon a large man was
at our house with boxes of tools. He opened the freezer, which
was stuffed with huge-quantity "good deal" items from Costco.

He turned to my wife and me. "Do you see what you've
done?" he asked, glaring at us accusingly, his stares alternating

between the freezer and us. We told him that no, we did not "see what we'd done."

"The freezer needs room for air to circulate. You've jammed it so full, it can't breathe. You've taxed its circulation system," he said harshly, as if we were bad parents who'd been feeding our children bacon fat for breakfast and lard for supper. "I'm glad I got here when I did; otherwise she might not be with us."

He was laughably serious. He turned to the freezer, where he removed about a third of the items and did some magic to restore it to health. As he gave us the bill he looked at us like he was a doctor who'd just revived a dead spouse, and said, "I love appliances. You two were lucky this time. I hope you'll learn from this and be more careful in the future." We thanked him, and as he left we felt as if the refrigerator had become our fourth child and we'd found the best pediatrician in the city.

I love meeting people who find joy in what they do. They've found a niche in this world, a skill or craft that resonates with how they're wired. I know mechanics, politicians, bus drivers, farmers, waiters, teachers, nurses, lawyers, parents, all sorts of people who are investing their lives in ways that resonate with who they're made to be.

Sadly, such joy remains the exception rather than the rule. Though there are thousands of ways we can paint hope on the canvas of this broken world, it falls to each of us to find the unique ways we're going to contribute; we aren't invited to contribute in a thousand ways but in a few very specific ways. Teacher, sculptress, waiter, lawyer, nurse, janitor, farmer, parent, poet, mentor . . . the list is endless, of course, and we need to figure it out, not just once, but for most of us several times during our lives.

This isn't just a matter of finding the right job. This is about how we invest all the waking hours of our lives. The fundamental challenge is that good lives are hard to come by because our days are vaporized by multiple obligations and trivialities, as if life is some sort of game, with everything coming at you, leaving you exhausted from reacting and trying to keep your head above water. Days turn into weeks, and years, and, presto—you look back and realize you never quite found the sweet spot where, as one of my favorite authors, Frederick Buechner, says, "the world's need and your deep joy intersect."

Finding our calling, our voice, is less like a treasure hunt and more like working the soil of a mysterious garden you didn't plant. As you do the soil care, eventually things come out of hiding, germinating and growing. "Aha! Those are strawberries!" This mystery garden is an apt metaphor, because for many of us our calling is hidden beneath the surface, buried under layers of phobias and ambitions, fears and failures. In spite of the soil called life that so often buries us, the truth is that with a little soul care, the seeds God put within us will germinate, thrive, and eventually bear fruit. Often, though not always, the fruit that comes won't be what we'd sought, intended, or anticipated—it will be better.

Caring for the soil of our souls requires, like good gardening, developing a few trusty habits.

KNOW

I grew up wanting to be an architect, and my dad's death while I was finishing high school only served to intensify that ambition. Seeing how short life might be, I determined to invest my days in creating monuments that would outlive me. Longing for immortality drove me as much as the love of space and texture, but whatever the motive, my path seemed obvious to me.

Then God stepped in. I'd headed off to a Christian ski retreat up in the mountains. A nice blonde was the main reason I made the trip, far more than Christ or skiing. God, however, didn't seem to worry about my motives for being there. Through the powerful words of a speaker who made me feel like I was the only one in the room, I encountered a challenge to make knowing God the highest and central pursuit of my life. It was there I discovered Jeremiah 9:23–27, which has become that little section in the Bible to which I return again and again when I'm feeling either confused, or weary, or overwhelmed, because it reminds me that the most important pursuit in my life is the pursuit of intimacy with God. It was there I knelt in the snow and prayed, committing to know God. It was there my plans began to unravel.

You'd think, or I would at least, that intimacy with God is the kind of pursuit that has precisely zero practical application, especially when it comes to matters of what to do for a living, and what to do with all those hours we have when we're done with our day jobs. Knowing God is about praying and reading the Bible, isn't it? Maybe, if you're mystical, it's about long, slow walks in labyrinths, or fasting, or silence; an occasional trip to a convent or monastery might come to mind as well. At the very most, all of it is supposed to make you do whatever it is you do, only better, with more of Christ's peace visible in your doing. That's what I always thought, anyway.

Turns out there's more to it. Knowing God has to do with learning about God's character, and developing a relationship with him, whereby God becomes real to us. Each morning I pour a pot of good French press coffee and meet with God. It's almost become a habit, like date night with my wife. And, like date night, I'm not consistent, with the plan sometimes giving way to other realities of life. Still, the relationship is important, and I find that by making time for meeting with God, marking it in my calendar, and showing up more or less regularly, my relationship with God becomes real.

As a result, "coffee with God" has become as vital to my spiritual health as time with my wife is to my marriage. There's listening, talking, expressing frustration and gratitude, and con-fession and forgiveness. There's laughter, response, questions, and frustrating silence. There's even the reality of my mind wandering or ignoring the other, when I ought to be listening; in other words, it's a lot like marriage, and for good reason.[1]

I'm convinced that this is the great starting point of finding our voice, our calling, because we're talking about becoming intimate with the One who created us and thus knows exactly what we're created to contribute to his good reign in this world. God knows what will energize us and what will suck us dry, and as we learn to live in relationship with him, we might just find our interests and aspirations changing, not because God sends us e-mails, but because spending time relating to him changes us.

After the ski retreat my relationship with God became much more real, and as it did, some strange things began happening: unanticipated, practical things, things that would change my life. The God I was getting to know began altering my longings and desires. Ever since kneeling in the snow that frigid night in the mountains and declaring my desire to know God, I found myself, oddly, less interested in architecture than before.

A little Bible study that a friend of mine taught in our dorm had caught on, growing from a handful of students to around fifty or more in a few short months. Lots of them didn't know much about Jesus when they started coming, but they were turning their lives in a new direction and getting baptized in the Pacific Ocean and reordering their lives around that of the Master Artist. It was quickly becoming my major point of interest, as the lives being changed were more exciting to me than physics and design courses. I still enjoyed the architectural craft of shaping living spaces (I still do—decades later). I just enjoyed playing piano for the Bible study and watching God change lives even more.

By the time I headed home for the summer, I had some serious doubts about whether I should continue studying architecture. I'd started thinking that maybe I could broker my music skills into some sort of life investing in people rather than buildings. By the end of the summer, I'd changed my major, changed colleges, and changed states. I moved to Seattle to study music composition and Christian education.

I hadn't set out, when committing to the goal of getting to know God better, to change the course of my vocational life. That shift was simply a byproduct, something that came out of my relationship with God. Like a good friend, he was rubbing off on me, and hanging out with him was having the unintended side effect of shifting my vocational priorities. Knowing God is soil care for the soul and, it turns out, has some very practical consequences.

YES

Fast-forward an entire year. I've moved from California to Seattle, fallen in love with rain, and am back home in California for the summer. I'm feeling very comfortable with my new major and can envision some sort of life unfolding where I'm making music for Jesus. Then something terrible happened: I taught a Sunday school class.

My youth pastor called on a Friday night and asked me to teach a Bible study for the high school group. This wasn't a difficult decision. "No thanks," I said, hung up the phone, and got on with my life. "Why would he think I'd be interested in teaching the Bible?" I asked myself, as I went back to shooting baskets above the garage. "Surely he knows how much I hated public speaking in high school?" I continued in my self-dialogue, recalling the nausea that threatened to erupt prior to each speech in that horrific class. I quickly dismissed the call as a joke of some sort.

Next morning. The phone rings again. It's the youth pastor. Same request, a second time. I tell him of my speaking phobia, assure him that he's misdialed, and get on with a morning of tennis and pizza. Back home, early afternoon, same phone, same guy, same request, but this time with two additional statements. "I'm calling again because I have this feeling that you're *supposed* to teach. I can't explain it. I just have this sense that you're the one for the job. And second, I'll be honest. I can't find anyone else."

Beaten down by his persistence and desperation, I relented. Only retrospectively do I realize that I was standing in the "yellow wood" of Frost's classic poem, where two roads converged. In saying yes to the road less traveled, I found that it *did* make all the difference. I found what I was made to do.

The first few steps on the teaching road, though, were as fun as a prostate exam. After agreeing to lead the class, I immediately panicked and regretted my poor refusal skills. Afterward I drove to my uncle's house and burst in, telling him how I'd been duped into teaching students at church in less than twenty-four hours, and how I would fail, dying a thousand deaths in front of merciless youths who would kill me with their blank stares or, worse, ignore me utterly as I tried to change their lives through teaching the Bible. When I'd emptied my soul and waited for a response, exposed, terrified, and broken, his eyes began smiling, and I thought he was maybe a sadist.

"I know just what you should teach!" he said, and without a hint of sympathy he disappeared down the hall, then came back with several fat books—"commentaries," they're called—on the Old Testament. My uncle, you see, is a pastor, and over the years I've come to discover pastors get all giddy when someone shows an interest in theology. Ask them for help in preparing a lesson and, well, let's just say that for a pastor, helping someone learn how to study and teach the Bible who's never done it before is about as satisfying as a fine steak and a good merlot (or whatever beverage your theology allows).

An hour later, armed with "observation, interpretation, correlation, application" (the code words for how to study the

Bible), I went home and opened the books. I don't know when it happened, but sometime after midnight, I noticed that the sense of dread had been evicted from my soul, replaced with a sense of genuine excitement to share the discoveries I'd made with the students. I could hardly sleep as I thought about how much fun it would be.

To say everything went smoothly would be an overstatement. All the phobias that caused me to say no in the first place made impressive showings, jumping in the car with me as I drove to church. Fear of rejection, fear of speaking, fear of being wrong, fear of being alone in front—they were all there. They sat in the back and reminded me of the reasons I wasn't cut out for this, which had to do with everything ranging from a poor body image, to abandonment issues, to my tendency to feel all the pain of worst-case scenarios before anything actually happens.

I went anyway, and the demons stayed in the car when I got out. By the end of the study on Joshua 1, I was sorry it was over, genuinely wishing I could do chapter 2 also.

Imagine my response when the youth pastor called late on Sunday and said he'd spoken to several students who wanted to hear what I had to say about Joshua 2, and could I show up again next week?

I taught the rest of the summer and eventually went to seminary because I wanted to gain more tools to teach better. I finished my course of study over twenty-five years ago and have been teaching the Bible ever since in many contexts all around the world. It's my greatest joy, by far. Every once in a while, the same condemning voices follow me into the classroom, or up to the podium, telling me I'm not charming enough, or smart enough, or have nothing to say. But I keep doing what I love doing and people keep showing up, to my amazement, to listen and learn. I've come to believe that the condemning, fear-inducing demons are lying.

Saying yes when asked to teach a class changed the course of my life. When we're in that season of life where we're looking for our voice, our unique creative niche, saying yes is vital, even when the opportunity is outside our comfort zone. Prior to that Sunday, I wanted to bless the world and serve God, but not by teaching the Bible or speaking in front of people. That was out of bounds, and I thought both God and I knew it. Maybe that's why the wisdom of old reminds us to "trust in the Lord with all your heart and do *not* lean on your own understanding."[2] My "own understanding" is why I said no to those initial invitations to speak, twice. Thank God the youth pastor was persistent, like parents who tell their kids to "at least try" the green beans. God won't *make* us do anything, but he'll grant us opportunities, through the chances to bless and serve the world that will come our way. Saying yes and showing up are often the biggest and hardest steps to finding our calling.

RISK

The problem, though, is that saying yes and trying different things means stepping into unknown realms. We're not going to find our voice without saying yes, trying some things, and failing. If this kind of vulnerability is to be avoided at all costs, we'll say no too often and run the risk of driving right past the "road less traveled," which, if we'd been more adventurous, would have enabled us to find our voice, our craft, our calling, and be a blessing to our world.

What gives a person the capacity to risk failure? This comes from having what I call a safety net, a place to fall down without destruction. God knows that failure will always bring with it a measure of rejection and self-doubt, but those with a safety net will somehow find a way to risk again, putting themselves out there on the front lines, because they believe that even in the worst-case scenarios of failure, their lives will still be intact.

Mountaineers understand the value of the safety net. When we're on a glacier, we're connected by a rope so that if one slips into the gaping jaws of a crevasse, the others will be able to protect him or her from free falling. Most of us, without the rope, simply wouldn't go. It's the same reason rock climbers belay each other and are linked. With the rope, there's still risk, but a slip of the hand or foot is no longer a risk of everything. We'll go places with a safety net that we simply wouldn't otherwise dare to venture.

When it comes to finding our calling and voice, the quality of our significant relationships seems to be what makes the net safe or unsafe. It's a great gift to be able to give our children enough affirmation that they can shoot for the moon and say yes to risk. All of us need this kind of safety net, but not all of us are fortunate enough to have it. Many are living under the threat of rejection and fear of failure, surrounded by toxic family relationships and friendships. How can such people learn to say yes, and risk?

This is, again, where God comes into the picture. In Psalm 73, Asaph makes this stunning declaration, referring to the sense of wholeness and completion he's found in God: "Whom have I in heaven but You? And besides You, I desire nothing on earth."[3] Though poetic hyperbole, the point is vital for our lives: Contentment in our relationship with God enables us to become people better able to cast out into unfamiliar waters. We know that in spite of the risks, we're never alone. The companionship of Christ becomes enough in very real ways as we navigate new waters, and this is vital, for it's in these new waters that we'll find the life for which we were made.

FAITH

> Without faith it is impossible to please Him, for he
> who comes to God must believe that He is, and that He is a
> rewarder of those who seek Him.[4]

In our tiny backyard are raised beds where we plant straw-berries, spinach, beans, and kale. Then there's the rest of the yard, which is more like a forest floor because of the giant redwood tree that canopies it, creating shade and a carpet layer of residue. We don't plant there, we don't till there; we don't expect edible vegetables there. We only till where we expect fruit, where we believe there are seeds.

Each of our lives is like that backyard. There's soil that will never grow anything meaningful and there is soil prepared for fruitfulness. The trick is in learning which soil is which and then, by faith, investing in the soil that will be fruitful. This is harder than it sounds because we live in a world that's telling us, over and over again in thousands of different ways, that truly barren soil will be fruitful if we'll but invest more in it. This messaging switches the price tags and tells us that we are what we own, or who we sleep with, or what we do for a living, or how much we weigh, or how clear our skin is, or what our family of origin has made us, or whatever.

These lies set us on journeys that will never bring content-ment, because the life for which we're created won't be found by tilling the forest floor of cultural consumerism, with its lusts for power, pleasure, and security. It will only be found in God's garden, and God tells us that he's placed his seed within us, particular good works for which we're uniquely gifted. Nurture the soil of your heart, and these are the seeds that will grow.

As these seeds germinate and we find our voice, we'll be stepping into the story God is writing, not just for here and now but for all eternity. As N. T. Wright says,

Every act of love, gratitude, and kindness; every work of art or music inspired by the love of God and delight in the beauty of his creation; every minute spent teaching a severely handicapped child to read or to walk; every act of care and nurture, of comfort and support, for one's fellow human beings and for that matter one's fellow non-human creatures; and of course every prayer, all Spirit-led teaching, every deed that spreads the gospel, builds up the church, embraces and embodies holiness rather than corruption, and makes the name of Jesus honored in the world—all of this will find its way, through the resurrection power of God, into the new creation that God will one day make.[5]

Finally, it's important to be reminded that these seeds of creativity and calling continue to sprout throughout our lives. A friend of mine left his work heading up a consulting company in order to take on the role of executive director at our growing church. A couple retire from their jobs, buy an organic farm in New Zealand, and use their guest houses on the farm to share the beauty of Christ through marvelous cooking and conversations about Christ and the environment. Another goes back to school in his late forties to become a teacher. A young man starts an economic development project in Uganda, and it becomes both a mission and a career.

How many stories do we need to hear before we begin to believe there are seeds still waiting to germinate? What are those seeds for you, for me? We'll only find out if we believe they are there and say yes to the habits of soil care that will enable them to grow.

10

OVERCOMING FAILURE

Finding Our Way to the Land of Grace

*We know that One is always and irrevocably for us, even
though what flows out of us when we listen to the voice of our
hearts gives evidence that we are not always for ourselves.*

–Doug Frank

*[We are not] adequate in ourselves to consider anything as com-
ing from ourselves.*[1]

–Paul the Apostle

Bryan is an artist and a teacher. He's been captivated by lots of
other endeavors over the years that we've been friends: he climbs,
plays soccer and the guitar, reads widely, rides mountain bikes and
road bikes. But Bryan always returns to art and teaching because
an artist and a teacher is what he is at his most fundamental level,
his way of painting hope on the canvas of our world.

He's taught art to middle-school students, which is a terribly challenging endeavor. If you think about it for a moment, you realize that before middle school, it seems everyone is an artist. When my now-grown children were young, I remember that each had creativity oozing out of them all the time. They managed to create whole worlds sometimes, like the time we went camping and they, lacking their home-turf toys, found a way to build a city from dirt, sticks, and pine cones. I remember watching my oldest daughter, foreman, architect, and general contractor, as she began to lay out the roads with her fingers, placing pine cone houses and stick cars strategically so that commerce could begin. Who taught her, at the age of seven, to view cities aerially? Where did she learn to imagine things into existence?

Then there was the time my youngest created the papier-mâché "Planet Bubba," along with commensurate stories about its populace and geography. My wife and I received homemade gifts of T-shirts with painted animals on them. Stick-figure drawings covered our refrigerator, probably yours too.

My son did art from the beginning, finding an ever-increasing voice and clarity through crafts like sculpture (we still have a blue head he made, strategically situated in our redwood tree) and photography. It was photography where he particularly excelled, his camera a frequent companion as he used subject, light, shadow, lens, and color to create beauty. Many rooms of our house display his handiwork, and his commitment to the craft eventually led him to study it extensively in college. He's found a creative niche.

Most aren't that fortunate. The prevailing norm is that our creativity disappears somewhere along the way, so that by the time we reach middle school, where Bryan teaches art, self-consciousness has displaced creativity. As a result, art is mixed with fear, tentativeness, and anxiety, rather than joyful creativity. These postures of heart might be fine for getting a root canal or colonoscopy, but they will kill our calling as artists. As a result, by the time most of us have celebrated our sixteenth birthday, we've stopped doing art.

I was curious about this, and asked my friend Bryan why people stopped creating. I thought it was probably just a simple matter of distraction, or too many sugary soft drinks. He explained that around age twelve or thirteen, our sensory perceptions outstrip our physical abilities. To put it another way, Bryan says, "When you're four, you can draw a circle, call it Grandma, and be okay with that. But by the time you're thirteen, you perceive that Grandma is more detailed than a simple circle. The problem is that even though you know this, you don't have the fine motor skills to draw her the way you know she looks. This gets frustrating for most students, to the point that they quit trying to draw at all. Why bother trying to a reach a goal if the trying leaves you falling short?"

We're on to something here, something that cuts to the very heart of how we live our lives of faith, and why so few are actively pursuing the creative adventure of spilling hope onto the world's canvas. The same dissonance between vision and fulfillment of vision that afflicts junior high art students afflicts most of us trying to follow Christ. It's not that we don't know what the Christian life ought to look like—it's that we know, but in spite of our knowing, we find ourselves unable to live it or create it accurately.

Once I started to see that the life to which Jesus was inviting me wasn't so much a life of prohibition as a life of invitation, I set out to become the kind of faith artist who paints hospitality and justice, love and generosity, boldness and hope.

The Bible is filled with good examples of this art, like the apostle Paul. There he is, unjustly accused and imprisoned, facing numerous delays and relocations for his multiple trials. Instead of sinking into a pity party as I'm sure I would, everywhere you find Paul he's praying for people, imparting hope, and telling God's story in such a compelling and inviting way that more and more people continue to step into it. Toward the end of his story, he's imprisoned in Rome and writes to some friends to tell them that this captivity has been a great blessing because it's opened doors of opportunity for God's good news to be declared in places of power that might never otherwise have heard. Written while he was chained to the Roman empire's equivalent of secret service agents, Paul's letter to Philippi makes it clear that several of those agents had decided to join God's story and become artists of hope. At the very end of this letter we discover that some members of Caesar's household had also joined, probably because they'd heard the message from the secret service, who'd heard it from an unjustly accused prisoner, who had faced death threats, shipwrecks, hunger, and beatings. I want to be impactful like that when *my* world is collapsing.

The trouble is, I can't even function well when I'm warm, full, and free. I can see Jesus, Paul, and others in the Bible living life the way it ought to be lived. To use Bryan's terminology, my sensory perceptions are increasingly attuned to the object I'm seeking to draw. I'm beginning to see, with increasing clarity, the life to which I'm called as a Christ follower, an artist of hope. But there's a dissonance between my perceptions and my capacities, or at least this appears to be so on the surface of things.

I know I'm called to hospitality, but at the end of a long day of work, I come home tired and grumpy. I don't even want to talk to my wife until I've disengaged from the real world by watching TV for a little while, no matter how inane the content. The thought of having people over is too much. "Not tonight" becomes almost a mantra as I settle into my isolated castle.

I know I'm called to generosity, but the economy has taken a terrible hit recently and there are no promises regarding the future, so rather than opening my wallet more generously as I've been blessed with resources, I sometimes tighten my grip instead. Fear of the future, though, is just a ruse sometimes.

The reality is that I want those resources in order to buy the stuff I've rationalized myself into believing I need (how can I truly engage in soul-winning conversations with my lift mates on the slopes if I continue to wear these embarrassing six-year-old skis?). I lay down the cash (metaphorically of course—it's really plastic) in exchange for whatever, and though I give to my church and elsewhere, I know that by any global standard I'm immensely wealthy. I could give more, should give more, live simpler.

This kind of dissonance reached an apex a couple of years ago when I was returning from a teaching trip in Europe. I'd just finished working carefully through the book of 1 Corinthians with a group of students in Austria. We were careful to spend some time on that famous part of the letter called "chapter 13," which declares that if we're not able to actively and demonstrably love other people, all our doctrinal propriety and zeal for God is a pile of garbage (my words, not Paul's, but that's the sense of it).

Because I'd used air miles for this trip, I had weird connections that required me to spend a few hours in the middle of the night in the Newark airport en route to Seattle. Being what Christians call "a good steward" (while the rest of the world calls it "cheap"), I'd decided to simply ride the trams all night instead of going to a hotel because I couldn't get past security until the next morning, when my airline issued my ticket for the final leg of my flight. So it's 1:30 AM. I'm alone when two large African-American teenagers board. My response is visceral. I immediately feel a quickening of my pulse, a tightening in my stomach. Out west, we've heard about Newark, and though I can't remember any details, something in my mind tells me that surely Newark leads the world in robberies and beatings of middle-aged white males in the middle of the night by African-American teenagers riding the tram at the airport.

I'm doomed, I think as I eye these two. I quickly determine

I'm going to wait and see if they're getting off at the next terminal, and if not, I'm going to jump out at the last second, just before the doors close. The plan comes off without a hitch. I've escaped!

It was there, though, that my faith unraveled. I sat there recalling how I'd just lectured on the primacy of love, how I'd just spoken so harshly of Christian racism in the American South, implying that we who lived far north of the Mason-Dixon line had the moral high ground. After all, we're in Seattle. I even have African-American friends. I'm an enlightened, double-shot Americano, upwardly mobile, highly educated Christ follower. Surely I've got it right.

"*Uh-huh,*" said a little voice inside my head as I sat on my backpack in the terminal, "except you were afraid of those two guys. You stereotyped them, got afraid, and ran. You talk a good game, but your words are a joke, bro. You don't live it, still, after all these years. You've still got racism rattling around in your soul." The voice was right, so far. But the voice didn't stop there.

"You're a pile of self-righteous crap, and the fact that you pretend to believe this stuff, and even have the guts to preach it, this just proves how rotten you are. You're actually a disservice to Jesus, and you'd be better off quitting." I could feel myself dissolving into a pile of condemnation. Artist? I'd seen the vision of just how beautiful reconciliation can be, had even preached about it often. But instead of drawing the fine lines of hope in that moment, I'd scribbled ugliness. I never wanted to paint again.

Have you heard the same condemning voice? Maybe you know the beauty of loving one's neighbor, know it as a concept at least. But the reality is that days turn into weeks, turn into months, and other than cursory hellos, these people who live so close you can pirate their Internet connection remain strangers. They've never seen the inside of your home and you don't know their stories at all. Or maybe you embrace the ideal of love and intimacy, then turn around and get your pleasure from pixels on a screen, treating the image like a human object that exists for your self-centered satisfaction.

The dissonance between the vision we've worked so hard to see clearly and the way we're actually painting our faith into the world is enormous, at least some of the time. This can be discouraging, devastating even. I know people who refuse to set goals or make resolutions because if they fail to keep them, they'll heap condemnation upon themselves, allowing a paralyzing sense of failure to so cripple their souls that any further growth and creativity becomes impossible.

Thankfully, the same "asterisk free" Paul who sets the example as an artist of hope offers guidance for the very real problem of the dissonance between Christ's vision for my life and how I'm actually living. Paul said in his letter to the Romans that he too has known this dissonance. The good things he wants to do, he doesn't do. The bad things he doesn't want to do, he does. He tries. He fails. He tries again and fails still again. This pattern continues on and on until finally, stuck in the Newark airport and existentially aware of what a loser he is, he cries out, "Wretched man that I am! Who will deliver me from this body of death?"[2]

The good news begins right there, actually, with his assessment that he's wretched. God knows that until we can come to the point of seeing our need for Christ's empowerment, we'll forever vacillate between the barren lands of either pride (where we think we've got this faith thing perfected) or condemnation (where once again we fail). We succeed. We fail. We try again, and succeed, and then fail, again. We. We. Or to personalize, "I. I. Me. Me." I need to get over myself. So when Paul says, "Who will deliver me?" his cry is good news in the sense that he's finally done trying to deliver himself, done trying to be Rembrandt when the reality is he has the artistic capacity of a tiny child.

When I see my efforts for what they are, I come to realize

there's Another who is more than willing to work with me, expressing his artistry through me, even through my most faulting and cumbersome efforts. The presence of this "Other," yoked with me as Lover, will be the source that perfects my art. I need to recognize this, and begin to believe it, for this is what it means to live as an artist on the basis of Christ's grace and power.

BEAUTY RISING FROM THE ASHES OF FAILURE

I'm not making this up. There's plenty of evidence, all through the Bible, that God is well able to use our tiny and faltering offerings; that he will, in his good time and plan, transform them into works of beauty. Take Judah, for example. His story would be the stuff of tabloids if he were in a famous family today.

His was and is a famous family—the original "first family" of God. The story goes something like this: God had chosen Abraham to leave his country and follow him to a new place where God would create a people whose lives would testify of the beauty, justice, generosity, and mercy of their Creator. These people would show the world what God is like, because they'd live in relationship with God, learning from him and following his plans and directions.

Things didn't quite work out that way. In fact, very quickly things turned sour, so that the twelve sons of Jacob, all great-grandsons of Abraham, could have occupied Dr. Phil's stage for an entire year with tales of theft, rape, deception, murder, and jealousy. We'll just look at one of many examples of failure.[3]

Judah has three sons, and his first son dies shortly after marrying a woman named Tamar. According to custom, Judah's next son is supposed to marry Tamar and produce offspring that would belong to his first son's "family." His second son, not liking the thought of this, practices a little coitus interruptus and "wastes his seed on the ground." God didn't like this, and the second son died instantly.

Judah was so self-righteous he decided Tamar was some sort of black widow, so he refused to let her marry the third son. Of course, he didn't share his true feelings but simply said his third son was too young. Days turned into years and it became apparent Judah was never going to allow Tamar to marry the third son. She decided to do something about it.

Judah's wife had died, and Judah was heading out on a business trip to a certain town. When Tamar heard about it, she dressed up like a prostitute and sat at the city gates as he approached. I always wonder how she knew that her father-in-law would be looking for a prostitute, and I have my theories, but not for publication. Anyway, like clockwork, he approached the customarily veiled Tamar in search of some recreation. They negotiated a price:

> "What will you give me?" she says.
> "I will send you a young goat from the flock," he says.
> "I want a security deposit."
> "What do you want?"
> "Your driver's license and credit card." (Okay, I'm making it contemporary. She wanted his staff and ring; both items were used for identification.)
> "Deal," he says, and they enjoy a romp in the prover-bial hay.
> When Judah later tries to recover his ID and pay her, the servant whom he'd sent with the payment comes back, saying, "I asked around but couldn't find her anywhere."
> "No problem," says Judah. "The whole thing will blow over soon enough."

Sometimes our mistakes do blow over, but not this time, because Tamar became pregnant that night. (Talk show headline:

"I'm carrying my father-in-law's baby, and he doesn't even know it, because when he slept with me I was disguised as a prostitute!")

When Judah hears the news—that Tamar is pregnant—he's incensed that his daughter-in-law is so trashy, has stooped so low. So he renders this verdict, as he's well able to do in his patriarchal culture: "Bring her out and let her be burned!" Apparently the thought never entered his mind that his life was just as tragic as hers. That's the way of it with self-righteousness: We become experts at seeing other people's trash with 20/20 vision while remaining utterly blind to our own.

That moment of clear seeing came later when, just before her executioners were set to light the fire, she sent a message to her father-in-law: "Tell Judah I'm pregnant by the man to whom these things belong." The messenger handed Judah his ID. Can you imagine the paradigm shift? Judah orders her released as it begins to dawn on him that he has his own issues, just like everyone else in this fallen world, issues with which he must deal. This is God's way of offering intervention.

The story doesn't end there, and maybe you're wondering, "What about the baby?" I should say *babies,* for Tamar had twins. The two boys born soon after that were named Perez and Zerah; shuffle through your Bible a few more books and you'll find a genealogy at the end of Ruth where we learn that Perez is the offspring through which God would eventually raise up a king named David, a king who represented God's heart quite well. Still in that same genealogical line, through David, one would eventually be born whose name is "Jesus—Emanuel—God with us."

When I first discovered this, a chill ran through my body, because I realized that God had taken a royal mess and transformed it into a thing of beauty. Eventually God would so transform petty, jealous, vengeful, lusting Judah that he would offer to let his youngest brother, who'd been framed for theft, go free, insisting that he would stay and serve out his days as a slave in foreign Egypt in his stead. That kind of life is first-class artistry, and it came out of the same man who slept with his daughter-in-law. Judah became the tribe of the kings, the line of Christ.

GOD KEEPS SHOWING UP—WE SHOULD TOO

Beauty can be born out of ashes, if we'll just keep showing up. Many don't, though. They grow tired of trying and failing. Those that stay with it begin to learn how to continue showing up, recognizing that our journey as artists isn't a matter of performance but partnership, whereby God takes our offerings of action and turns them into works of art.

Fortunately, God has ways of helping us learn this lesson. I'd been a Christian for nearly thirty years and in ministry for more than ten when I was invited to speak at a men's conference. I don't know what was happening to me, but the week leading up to the conference wasn't good. I'd experienced a run-in with my wife and some stresses in my ministry. I'd been working too many hours and was tired. To top it off, I'd been neglecting the disciplines of which I spoke in my previous book[4] and so was running on fumes spiritually.

The truth of the matter is that even the fumes were gone by the time I reached the conference. You see, on the flight there, I'd sunk into a state of heart that could only be described as ugly. Some self-pity was there, along with some pride, along with a little bit of coveting, and a few other things that aren't exactly godly.

When I arrived at the retreat center I was in a thoroughly foul mood and didn't even want to speak to the men who'd paid good money and traveled some distance for this event. I was in my room having a pity party. The director knocked on my door: "The guests are arriving."

In my politest voice possible I said, "I'll be there soon," which was code for "*I wish I wasn't here. I wish you'd leave me alone. I wish I were a better person. I wish I were qualified to speak at this retreat. I don't want to talk to you. I don't want to talk to a roomful of men about a God who feels utterly absent to me right now.*"

He couldn't interpret my code, though, because when the singing began, he knocked once more and said, "After this song I'll need to introduce you," which was his code for, "*I'm paying you to show up, Dahlstrom! The very least you can do is actually show up!*"

So I did. I went out, carrying my Bible, feeling like the biggest hypocrite on the planet, and listened to an introduction of myself that I found hard to believe, because I knew myself better than the guy introducing me knew me. But I smiled and stood, and then there was another song, during which I prayed, *God, what am I doing here, teaching the Bible, when my heart is filled with all this darkness? I feel bad for these guys who think they are coming to hear someone who is living his faith well, whose heart is completely given to you, whose words match all his actions, not just his public persona. God, I'm so sorry I've let you down.* I prayed all of this before I rose to speak, while the men were singing and then praying for me.

Then I got up and began to teach my series, from the book of John, and that night I was talking about how Jesus turned water into wine. I was sharing with the guys that the wine represented blessing, fullness, joy, and that this couple had run out of it and was in danger of humiliating themselves at the outset of their married lives. I'm listening to myself talk, and I'm realizing that I too am out of wine, that I too am in danger of humiliating myself in front of these very good people who have come to hear something from God through me.

So I went on to explain how the next step would be to make ourselves available to Jesus like the people responsible for the wine at the wedding did. They wouldn't get a lecture about poor planning, like they might from a typical parent. Instead, Jesus would intervene on their behalf and salvage things, bringing blessing where it wasn't deserved, because that's exactly what Jesus does.

I finished my talk, bowed my head to lead in prayer, and said, "There are some of us in the room tonight who know that the joy has dried up, that the blessing has dried up, that there's no wine. But we've shown up. And because of that, Jesus can bring a work of transformation. And I'm going to pray for that transforming work right now." Then I prayed, and when I opened my eyes, men were weeping and hugging each other. I would later learn that two churches involved in a split had both signed up for this conference, each without knowing the other would be there, and that my talk that night was the beginning of a work of restoration and reconciliation.

However, I'd be lying if I said the whole event pleased me. In truth, I went back to my room and complained to God, pointing out that it was not fair of him to use me when I was behaving like a spiritual fraud. I like formulas. I like a payout when I've been good, and punishment when I've failed. That way I can look at everything that's happening and know if I'm a good or a bad boy. But God reminds me over and over again that it's not about me. It's about God and God's grace. He'll use a rock if he needs to. He proved it once again that night.

It's as if, when I was done ranting, God said, "Thanks for that. Richie . . . do you remember your dad letting you pitch, cheering you on even though you'd shattered the living room window at home? Do you remember the root beer floats the Little League coach bought even when you guys lost, the lessons you learned about love? You do? Great! Then maybe you remember this little bit that I wrote: 'What man is there among you who, when his son asks for a loaf, will give him a stone? Or if he asks for a fish, he will not give him a snake, will he? If you then, being evil, know how to give good gifts to your children, how much more will your Father who is in heaven give what is good to those who ask Him!'[5] Do you remember that?"

I did, and I do still. Though the dissonance between God's vision for my life and the reality of my paltry capacities and offerings still rears its head on a regular basis, I'm learning to relax and keep showing up, thanking God in advance that he can take my offerings and turn them into masterpieces because of his power and grace.

As a result, I'm a child again, not afraid to paint, not afraid of the dissonance between who I am and who I'm becoming. The journey's become much lighter as a result.

OBSTACLES AND RESISTANCE

The Artist as Warrior

*How many of us have become drunks and drug addicts, devel-
oped tumors and neuroses, succumbed to painkillers, gossip, and
compulsive cell-phone use, simply because we don't do that thing
that our heart is calling us to?*[1]

—STEVEN PRESSFIELD

*He who would learn to fly one day must first learn to stand and
walk and run and climb and dance; one cannot fly into flying.*

—FRIEDRICH NIETZSCHE

We'd purchased the property. It was five acres deep in the Cascade Mountains and included a large three-story chalet as well as
five small cabins. The vision was simple: provide a place where
people can receive teaching and hospitality, sharing truth and
life at the same time. The vision was born in a time when TV
preachers were giving God a bad name by talking about purity

while the preachers themselves were having multiple affairs, calling people to generosity while being discovered as greedy tax evaders. My wife and I were sick of the disconnect, so with another couple we'd prayed about this vision. And when the property opened up, we tossed our life savings into the kitty for a down payment and made an offer.

Amazingly, the sellers chose us over other offers, a choice that had nothing to do with our wealth and everything to do with our vision, which somehow resonated with them. It appeared this move from our island home to the mainland was going to happen.

It's just that I thought the move would happen later than it did. Sure, we had this vision to practice the arts of hospitality and teaching, but there were some practicalities to consider. My wife was pregnant with our third child, and we'd invested everything in the down payment, so it seemed prudent to live frugally for at least a year or two and save up some kind of cushion before venturing into these waters.

I'll spare you the details, but things didn't unfold along such a safe and predictable path. Instead, within a few short months of buying the place, we moved off the island, away from the security of a small but consistent paycheck. We had no savings, no visible means of support, and no clear sense of how we were going to pay our way.

To top it off, we moved in on December 11, and on December 17, a once-in-a-century storm blew through, knocking down seventeen trees on our property and killing the power, with wind gusts over 100 miles per hour snapping the frozen trees like matchsticks (only later would we learn that we'd moved to a region called "Windy Flats"). The temperature was hovering around 0°, but the wind-chill readings were double digits below that. Lacking power, my family, recently grown to a total of five with the addition of our then six-month-old daughter, was trying to preserve warmth by sleeping huddled together in sleeping bags, in front of the woodstove.

Sleeping is the wrong word, though, because the house sounded like it was going to blow apart, and shortly after midnight a bright spotlight began shining in our window. I rose from my bag and staggered through the house, which was holding its own in toasty 45° warmth. There was a truck parked in our driveway. I put on several layers and ventured out to see who they were; turns out they were county rescue people.

They said, "We're trying to decide whether to send people who've lost their homes over here to your house, or get you guys out."

"Why would we need to leave?" I asked.

"That big cedar tree in front of your house? If it goes, your chalet will be history and you'll probably become casualties of the storm."

We chatted until I felt like my lips were going to drop off, and they decided our place was neutral—too risky to invite others over, not risky enough to force us to leave. I went back inside and lay awake through the rest of the night, wondering. We *thought* we'd heard the voice of God calling us, thought the signs had all pointed in this direction, thought that once we stepped out in obedience and did the right thing, the pathway would open up for us and we'd watch miracles happen.

Oops. Instead I'm lying awake while my family tries to stay warm in a house at risk of being blown apart or crushed, and I've no visible means of supporting any of them into the foreseeable future. Either I've been listening to the wrong voices (delusional voices, naïve voices, voices filled with romantic notions of mountain life), or the right Voice doesn't like me after all and has brought me and my family out here to kill us. I spent the night walking back through the pages of my life, highlighting every bit of lust, greed, complacency, and fear of which I could think. By first light I was amazed we were all still alive and was already trying to figure out how to leave this place and get a real job.

Instead of quitting, though, like I wanted to that night, we stayed for nearly seven years. And they were good years—very good. Our family looks back on those days in the mountains as some of the richest in our lives, both as a family and as artists of hope. Not only did we survive the storm, but we saw the next morning that, in spite of all the trees that had snapped like twigs and fallen all over the property, none of them touched either the chalet or the cabins. Our cars were spared too, our little diesel Rabbit having been crisscrossed by fallen fir trees over a foot in diameter, without leaving a scratch on the vehicle.

We had the big cedar tree felled; turned out that it was rotten to the core and *should* have blown down. The logger, who later become a good friend and a board member for our mountain ministry, said there was no way that tree should still be standing, except for the "act of God" clause, which, it turns out, can be applied to good news as well as bad. Right in the midst of the storm (or at least, right after it) we saw evidence of God's hand upon us and all over the property.

THE WAY IT REALLY IS . . .

We'd like to think that obedience to God, following our passions, and finding our voice will mean that the path opens up for us marvelously, clearly, without a hitch. I'm not sure why we like to think that way, because even a casual glance at the Bible paints a completely different picture of the road toward becoming an artist of hope.

Abraham obeys God, then doubts, agonizes, lies, and sleeps with his maid in order to impregnate her before fully following. Joseph has a vision for ascendancy and ruling but then finds himself sold into slavery and framed for rape. David is anointed king, then needs to go into exile to survive. Jeremiah follows his calling and receives mockings, beatings, and imprisonment as a result.

Let's not forget about John the Baptist. He's the one who, when he first saw Jesus, cried out with confidence, "Behold, the Lamb of God who takes away the sin of the world!"[2] He knew that this was the One; knew that Jesus must increase but John must decrease, knew that Jesus' greatness was such that he wasn't even worthy to untie Jesus' sandals.

In spite of this confidence, a day comes when he's full of doubt and discouragement. Two disciples visit John in prison and he says to them, "Go and ask Jesus if he's the Messiah or if I should be waiting for another." Reading between the lines, it's not hard to understand John's question. "If Jesus is the Messiah, if he really is beginning a new reign and a new world, then what am I doing here, rotting away in prison? After all, I'm only here because I called Herod out on his immorality, called him to follow your will, Jesus, called him to the ethic of your reign. I did the right thing, and this is the thanks I get? Maybe I'm missing something, or maybe you're not the Messiah."

It's vital to understand that finding our voice and calling isn't some sort of ticket to bliss and ease in the days that follow. To the contrary, it seems that once we set our hearts on stepping into our part of the story God is writing, all the forces of hell will set themselves against our progress.

Take the Old Testament story of Joshua and Caleb. They stood apart from their contemporaries because they were the only ones willing to follow through on the vision God had imparted. God had invited Israel to enter a brand-new land and set up shop in it. He'd said it would become a place where his character would be on display for all the world to see, so that others from other nations could see the beauty of his reign and join the party. This new land would be a place of justice, peace, abundance, and hospitality.

It all sounded marvelous, but when the day came to actually make the move, these two were voted down, the initiative defeated 10 to 2. All twelve agreed with the vision, agreed it was good, worthy, and hope-filled. Most of them just didn't think it worth the risk and hassle. Easier to keep with the status quo, or even go back to slavery.

I'm guessing the ratio of no to yes votes is still about the same today, and that's why there are so many schools and clinics yet to be built, paintings yet to be created, songs yet to be sung, books yet to be written, works of hope yet to be done. It's not a shortage of vision; it's a shortage of moving into the vision and making sure it happens.

Between vision and fulfillment there's always some resistance. Seeing it, naming it, and doing battle with it is an art form in itself. It's that art form to which we now turn our attention, and the first, perhaps biggest form of resistance that needs addressing is named *procrastination*.

TODAY

We don't even know how to say this guy's name, let alone read his contribution to the Bible. Haggai is a tiny book tucked away toward the end of the Old Testament, between Zephaniah and Zechariah. Thumbing through the Bible, you'd probably not even see it. Little wonder, then, that so many of us miss the life-changing principles contained in it.

Haggai was around at a time when Israel was coming into the land from which they'd been exiled. Their temple and city walls had been destroyed nearly one hundred years earlier, but now some people were finding their way home. As a nation, they had a vision to rebuild God's temple and had begun to do so shortly after returning.

Quickly, though, they'd run into resistance. A group of people, fearful that the rebuilding project would incite nationalism, which would potentially lead to civil unrest and rebellion, had acquired a sort of "stop work" order for the project. This had the effect of killing momentum, and the enthusiasm and vision for rebuilding died quickly.

But it didn't just die for a day, or a week, or months. When Haggai came on the scene, the foundation had been sitting there for more than fifteen years! People had started walking in the vision but quit when the resistance kicked in, and people got on with their lives, as other matters displaced the vision that had once occupied their hearts and minds.

Haggai comes on the scene, sees the incomplete building as an embarrassment, and confronts the community. Their response is perhaps one of the most insightful passages anywhere for we who are trying to fulfill our callings as artists of hope: "The time has not come, even the time for the house of the LORD to be rebuilt."[3]

There's the subtle and supremely deceptive power of procrastination at work, in all its despicable glory. The people didn't say, "Temple? Listen, old man, we gave up on that nonsense a long time ago and decided to get on with our tiny, boring, consumerist lives, occupying ourselves with nothing more than getting our piece of the pie and preserving it from thieves. Forget it, Haggai, and leave us alone."

That would have been so much easier to deal with, because it would have been more honest. But such honesty, because it leads to the kind of profound conviction that can shake us out of complacency, is rare. Instead, we paint a layer of holy veneer on our procrastination by saying, "Of course we want to rebuild the temple (or write the book, paint the picture, fix our marriage, reconnect with our children, have neighbors over for supper, work in the orphanage, teach English to immigrants, care for AIDS victims, work in the homeless shelter . . .). And we will someday. Just not today."

Haggai's hearers offer a litany of excuses for failing to be artists of hope, all prefaced with the little phrase "as soon as." Reading between the lines, you can see that they're saying, "As soon as we finish remodeling our houses. As soon as we've saved up enough money. As soon as we bring the crops in. As soon as we get ahead a bit financially." We all know the drill, each of us having our own "as soon as" excuses that enable procrastination.

Haggai sees it differently, though. In essence he says, "If you're waiting until you're secure enough, certain enough, free enough, comfortable enough to begin your calling as an artisan of hope, I've news for you: you'll wait forever." He's right, of course. There's always a reason not to begin. We had an infant and no money when it was time to move off the island and start a new work in the mountains. It was a time of financial uncertainty, a time of utter dependency on God, a time of challenge because we didn't have all the answers for all the questions people were asking us about this new work—and in the midst of all that uncertainty, it was also the right time to move.

Please hear me. I'm not advocating irresponsibility, or reckless spontaneity. Our move off the island and into the mountains came with blessings and encouragement, from both the leaders of our church on the island and the board of our new ministry. Everyone agreed: it was time to move. We were afraid, because we'd never done anything like this before, because we didn't know how it would turn out, because failure was a real possibility. And we moved. Sometimes we need to ask this very simple question regarding our calling as artisans of hope: "What are we waiting for?"

PERSEVERANCE

Scott and Pam are two of our best friends in Seattle. They started a theater company called Taproot in 1976 and have been blessing their city with quality drama ever since. They've seen other theater companies with similar visions come and go at various locations in North America, but theirs, in a city that's antagonistic to the gospel, is thriving, blessing believer, seeker, and secularist alike. The four of us sat down over a good meal recently in a mountain log cabin and talked about our respective ministries, and what continuity looks like as vision is born and matures. As the candles drew low and rain pelted the roof, they recounted how about every seven years, their theater company would once again find itself at a major crossroads. Each time, they'd revisit their identity and calling as artists of hope. Each time, they'd decide to continue.

After the first seven years of their fledgling company, Scott and Pam realized that if things continued on their present course, they'd never be able to have a family. The time, money, and energy needed for raising children weren't available because their vision demanded everything. They were exhausted and ready to quit, but their board said, "If you quit, we'll need to close up shop, because this work won't continue without you."

Independently, they took some time to consider their calling and their future. "The two of us came to the same conclusion," Pam recounted, "separately deciding that if Taproot's mission wouldn't continue without us, we weren't done." Scott added that both of them came to this conclusion for the same reason: "Because the mission, 'to create theater that explores the beauty and questions of life and offers hope in our search for meaning,' was still unfulfilled. The work still needed to be done."

Anything worth doing is going to draw on our limited resources of energy and time, and those two precious commodities are going to be taken from some other area of our lives. The ongoing decision to continue this reallocation is one of the ways we all must face "the resistance," whether we're starting a theater company, writing a book, raising a family, cooking healthy food, or trying to educate poor children in the inner city. When we're in the midst of battling the resistance, we'll often feel a tension between vision and resource, and it's this tension that has the effect of testing the depth of vision, especially when things don't open up remarkably, or easily, or according to our timetable.

Our early days in the mountains were filled with extra work for income sources, ranging from officiating basketball games, to renting out cabins to travelers, to writing and administering a grant for our county. These were day jobs, and the rest of the time we devoted to our arts of hospitality, teaching, and raising three young children. "Whatever it takes" became our mantra, because there was a fire in our bones, a passion to see teaching linked with hospitality, to share with people not only content but actual life; that was the art to which we were called.

The main things to which we're called are the "big rocks" of life. Denis Haack, founder of Ransom Fellowship, taught me years ago that you need to put the big rocks in the cup of life first, which means you need to know what those rocks are. As Simon Sinek points out in his book *Start with Why*, the Wright brothers and Steve Jobs and Martin Luther King Jr. all share something in common. In spite of resource shortages and multitudes of naysayers, they became leaders at the forefront of culture-changing innovations, and all of them for the same reason: They knew the answer to the question *Why?* They had clear vision regarding how machine-powered flight, or personal computers, or civil rights would change the world. They weren't after fame. They had fire in their bellies, a compulsion to invest all their resources in their vision. They knew "why" this was to be their particular contribution to the canvas that is our world. They'd found their big rocks.

Once you find the big rocks, you can fill in the leftover space with smaller rocks. If you reverse the order, you'll never find space for the big rocks. This is a battle because the little rocks of e-mail and sitcoms, sporting events and net surfing will suck the life out of us, leaving us no time or energy for our calling. Sometimes, even fitting all the big rocks into the cup can be a challenge.

MULTIPLE ROLES

We're always more than our art, more than our vocation, more than relationships. We're all of these things, and more, at the same time. This becomes a problem at times, because we're left feeling that whatever it is we're doing, we're not giving it as much as we could, and so we think how much better we'd be if only there were more time.

I don't write for a living, because I have a different day job, leading and serving an urban church. This consumes most of my time, and though I love it, the realities of that role limit the possibilities of other roles. I'm also a father to three grown children, a husband of one great wife, and an occasional teacher at conferences, churches, and Bible schools.

Because of these multiple roles, I stare at paragraphs just like this one and get discouraged, thinking, *You could be a better writer if you spent more time with the craft.* I think the same thing about my role as parent, and my teaching ministry in the church and elsewhere, and my relationships with my neighbors, and my rock-climbing hobbies. On my worst days, all of them feel thinly executed, and I beat myself up over how much better I could be. How do I find balance between all the roles? How do any of us?

This was another subject Scott and Pam broached the other night. As their ministry matured they eventually had two marvelous children. Pam was working for the theater part time, acting in plays and raising kids, so that the balancing act was in full swing. If you've ever walked on a slackline or a tightrope, or ever gone rock climbing, you know that balancing, at its busiest, can be exhausting. Pam put it well: "You fall in love with these babies. You fall in love with their world. And because of this, the actor part of you that requires immense amounts of time and discipline gets torn in different ways."

She recalled a time when she was feeling pulled in lots of directions. Her daughter, Lisa (now an adult), was excited about her ballet recital, but when Pam went to mark it on the family calendar, she suddenly realized she was going to miss it because she was in a play. Even though Dad would be there, and Grandma would be there, and lots of other extended family would be there, this realization melted her, and she found herself crying in the kitchen over the loss, wondering if the roles of parent, actress, and administrator were all doable when rolled into one person.

It was her eight-year-old son, Peter, who offered the inspiration and guidance. He asked, "Mommy, what's wrong?" She told him Lisa had a recital and that she'd painted herself into a corner with too many obligations, that she would miss her daughter's recital, that it was all too much. Peter's answer was simple and straightforward: "You're a better person when you do plays, Mommy." I love it when our children counsel us.

That was what she needed to hear, and there's a sense in which it's what all of us need to hear because all of us have more than one role to play in this world, more than one rock in our cup. We need to be reminded that sometimes we'll be focusing on one rock more than another, and that's okay. All of us have gifts (plural) to offer. What's more, from season to season even these big rocks will change in both size and priority. Children are a larger rock in your cup when you're homeschooling them than when they're thirty (usually). Marriage, work, your craft and gifts, relationships with friends—each element has a season when it's the biggest rock of all, and it will require wisdom to weigh the rocks and put them in the right place.

Romans 12 reminds each of us that as we live out from the storehouse of wisdom God gives us, we'll learn to think more accurately about ourselves. To put it personally, I'll stop wasting my time trying to be a vocal soloist or climbing big walls in Yosemite because, though I might want to do both, my finite resources of time and the way I'm wired mean I'd be wise to spend this time elsewhere. I'm a teacher, leader, writer, husband, pastor, dad, neighbor, son. It appears my plate is full, even without big-wall climbing.

Wisdom pushes us, though, even a step further than simply knowing how we're wired and knowing the "why" of our calling. Wisdom means our decision-making on any given day or moment is going to be situational and relational rather than formulaic. Pam acted in the play rather than going to her daughter's recital. I'm skipping date night this week because I'm hiding in a cabin in order to finish this book, using some precious vacation days to do it. I've backed out of speaking engagements in the past because of big moments in the life of our church that demanded my attention. I've taken afternoons off to go skiing with my kids.

THE THINGS WE KEPT THROUGH THE FIRE

In autumn 2009, an arsonist started burning buildings down in the neighborhood of Taproot Theatre. One of the company's buildings burned to the ground, and the theater building itself suffered extensive water damage as firefighters fought valiantly to save it from the flames. In the end, it was shut down for three full months for the repairs and restoration work required to reopen.

If I consider their response as a snapshot of their calling at the thirty-five-year mark and contrast it with their seven-year mark, I learn about the priceless value of overcoming the resistance and pressing on as artisans of hope. We talked about the fire several months after it happened, and Scott said, "I was standing in the rain watching the building burn down at 5:30 in the morning. The whole staff was there by 8:30, and immediately we just started talking about next steps: What are we going to post on the website? What about the show that's tonight? What about the upcoming Christmas show? There was never a question of quitting. The whole staff was standing there and by their actions were saying, "We're in it for the long haul. The building is only a building, not who we are."

Seattle Children's Theatre offered their space so Taproot could complete the final performances of the show running at the time of the fire. Another organization stepped up to provide space at their location for the thirty-five performances of Taproot's holiday production. Taproot paid the actors and actresses for the performances that needed to be cancelled. They put on two shows after reopening on a "pay what you can afford basis" with all proceeds going to the Greenwood Fire Fund. They've continued to receive feedback from granting agencies and other theaters about how inspiring their navigation of the fire, rebuilding, and reopening has been.

I think an important key to all this, also, is what Scott said about their truest calling. "We were Taproot," he said, "when all we owned was five stools in the back of our Toyota." In other words, they've been securing their calling as artisans of hope by faithfully serving and perfecting their craft day after day, regardless of accolades or the lack thereof. That, it seems to me, is what each of us needs to do if we're going to mature into the people of blessing we're called to be.

Artisans of hope bless the world most profoundly right in the midst of the fire. That's because the fire reveals who we really are, and who we really are isn't created in the crisis. It's created on those boring Tuesdays when it would be easier to blow off our calling than do the inglorious work of showing up with a paintbrush in front of a canvas, or with medicine in front of a sick baby, or with a shovel in front of a compost pile, or with a pen in front of a law brief, and whatever you're called to do. Practice your craft with integrity. Nobody's even looking, let alone thanking you. But your soul is being shaped, and when the time is right, that well-crafted soul will be used to bless the world as you paint just the right stroke of justice, mercy, and intimacy, in just the right place.

12

CHANGE

Grappling with the Preacher of Chair 8

Just because everything is different doesn't mean anything has changed.

    —IRENE PETER

We did not change as we grew older; we just became more clearly ourselves.[1]

    —LYNN HALL

We would rather be ruined than changed
We would rather die in our dread
Than climb the cross of the moment
And let our illusions die.

    —W. H. AUDEN

THE CHAIR 8 INTRUDER

Good days for skiing are rare in the Cascade Mountains of Washington State. Snow's not a problem. There's plenty of that from Halloween through Memorial Day, or even Independence Day some years. But there aren't many days when you can see. All that snow, after all, needs to come from somewhere. Our reputation as a cloudy, depressing place to live is well earned, at least with respect to the cloudy part. Three hundred or more days a year we're sheltered from the nastiness of UV rays because the sun is hiding behind a thick layer of clouds blowing in off the mighty Pacific. Mount Baker ski area boasted over a thousand inches of snow one year (that's about eighty-three feet, for the non-mathematical). You don't get that kind of snowfall with only a dozen snowy days per winter punctuating a sun festival. No sir. You get that kind of snow when it falls from the sky constantly for weeks on end.

I was planning a personal retreat time up near Mount Baker when I awoke one morning in the retreat cabin, a mere half hour from the ski area, to clear skies. Blue is a seductress in the Northwest, and when she lifts her grey skirt even a little, many are powerless to resist. We're lured away from work, worship, and yes, even personal retreat days that were to be devoted to prayer and planning.

Since it was Wednesday, and nobody expected this kind of ridiculous sunshine, I parked my car right there with the other thirty or so others, bought my lift ticket, and began my prayer retreat in the solitude of a nearly empty ski area. No lines. Perfect snow. Blue sky. Silence. Spectacular beauty.

Somehow, the synapses between brain and muscle were firing well too, so that I was skiing at my capacity, nailing turns, conquering powder. It was pure exhilaration, one of the great days of my life. For the first hour of the day my only regret was that I wasn't sharing it with anyone; wife, children, friends, everyone had more important things to do. Joys are better shared, but when I called my wife at her work from the chairlift she wasn't cheered by the news of perfect snow, blue sky, and no lines. Her office doesn't even have a window. Her chastening was enough for me to forget about being alone and just enjoy the day. I jumped in, skied hard, celebrated the beauty, and gave thanks for my health. It was a nearly perfect morning.

But then, after lunch, I was riding up chair 8 and something happened that I'll never forget. From somewhere, the thought came to me that this kind of enjoyment in life is fleeting at best. It was almost as if a voice outside of myself was speaking to me: *"Go ahead and enjoy this day, Richard, because the odds of it ever happening again are slim. And even if through some miraculous convergence of good fortune it were to happen again, and even again still after that, the day of your own demise will come eventually. The day will come when you'll not be able to do this anymore. This pleasure is fleeting, ephemeral, vaporous; it can't be captured."*

I could feel the melancholy descend on me, right there alone on the lift. There was something aching in me, some longing that this kind of beauty and joy be permanent, not fleeting, universal, not the endowment of a privileged minority. And I knew this wasn't the case. I knew the voice speaking was telling the truth. I'd seen it too many times to deny it. There are pictures of my dad running track in college in a scrapbook. By the time I was in high school, he couldn't walk to the bathroom without the help of an oxygen tank attached to him. My father-in-law taught me to ski. He spent the last years of his life with dementia, sometimes not even recognizing his own family, barely able to walk.

I tried to push away the whole nasty "voice of reality" by skiing black diamonds. Shoot, make it a double. But as soon as I got back onto the lift at chair 8, the voice continued preaching. *"Forget about yourself for a minute, Rich. Think bigger still. See those trees you love, white clad today, vibrant in their beauty? You like to think about how the Bible speaks of them clapping their hands in praise. You're reminded of that on those windy days when you're backpacking. I know. It's true. It's also true that every tree you see will also disappear, just like you. In fact, the chair lift you're riding will be gone too someday. If you're going to try and hang on to the present, my friend, you're setting yourself up for a life of grave disappointment. Everything ends. Deal with it."*

I stopped riding chair 8 for the rest of the day, fearful that perhaps the ghost of chair 8 had another sermon to preach. I was tired of these harsh doses of reality. But when I arrived back at the cabin that evening, after bathing away my soreness and cooking a nice meal, I sat and read through the book of Ecclesiastes, suspecting that the preacher of chair 8 was not just a voice inside my head while riding up for those runs, but was perhaps the author of that book in the Bible too. When I'd read it in seminary I'd found it a little depressing. It reminded me of the voice I'd heard earlier in the day.

Yes, there it was:

> A generation goes and a generation comes, but the earth remains forever. . . . That which has been is that which will be, and that which has been done is that which will be done. So there is nothing new under the sun. . . . There is no remembrance of earlier things; and also of the later things which will occur, there will be for them no remembrance among those who will come later still.[2]

EVERYTHING CHANGES

That particular day was just one of at least several hundred in my life that I, given the opportunity and omnipotence to do so, would have frozen for all eternity to enjoy.

Look, there I am sitting in my dad's lap, wrapped in his overcoat on a cold San Francisco night at a baseball game. Only my head is sticking out, because the wind and fog have turned this summer night into the big chill. But I don't care because I'm warm, Willie Mays is in center field, Mom and Dad are having the time of their lives, and there's hot chocolate for all of us.

There I am lying on the trampoline, watching the clouds go by with my youngest daughter. She's identifying them: Winnie the Pooh, a turtle. She hugs me and says, "I never want to leave home." Why can't this last forever?

Why indeed. Can't we take the innocence of childhood, the strength of youth, the wisdom of old age, the romanticism of new marriage and simply freeze them so they don't change? Isn't there a pill for that? Of course, that was the point the preacher of chair 8 was making that day on the slopes; we can't freeze our glimpses of glory. They show up, like slides on your screensaver, and then they're displaced by other pictures. This reality of incessant change, of course, colors the entire canvas of our lives, and our world.

The truth is there are constant changes in both the world and the roles we play as child, spouse, parent, worker, friend, and neighbor. Just when we become friends with our neighbors, they move away. When we finally get this marriage thing figured out, pregnancy arrives. By the time we master the skills required to be good parents, our children know more than we do and move out of the house. All the while, our bodies and pocketbooks are changing, for better or worse. And though there are great moments along the way, they too shall pass. Like a river, our lives are the product of a constant flow of input, output, beauty, ugliness, failure, grace, strength, and aging, so that though we are always who we are, we are never who we were yesterday.

Step back from our personal situations a bit, and we realize all of these micro changes occurring in our own lives are happening in a macro sea of change. A new treatment-defying disease brings an entire continent to the brink of disaster and exposes our need to change how we think and talk about sex. There are economic cycles of boom and bust, as well as the wars and rumors of wars that characterize at least some decades for every generation. I woke up on September 10th, 2001, thinking that my biggest problem was how to prepare for the annual meeting at our church the next night. Within twenty-four hours, the whole world had changed: a new kind of war, a new kind of enemy, a new kind of wisdom needed, all in the wake of shattered innocence as two planes crashed into two towers. Oil becomes scarce. Water is next. House prices change, and buying habits change. New generations arise, whose entire view of the world is dramatically different, and they bring their ideas with them into the workplace, and yes, even into church. Our protective bubbles have been popped.

Romantic notions that life can attain to some sort of stasis must die. In their place, we need to develop a perspective that enables us to be adaptable people, forever learning, forever adjusting, so we can continue to be the artisans of hope Jesus intends us to be.

Too often the reality is that change buries us. We're paralyzed by grief, like the man who never played music again after his wife died, or the artist who refused to paint after losing his son.

For others, it's not change itself that kills our artistic spirit; it's the fear of change. Desperately wanting to hang on to today as a freeze frame, we spend all our energy trying to stay young, or stay rich, or stay wherever it is we've decided we need to stay in order to keep doing what we're doing.

A TIME FOR EVERYTHING

"I wonder if I can find some decent examples of people who've kept up their craft, continued their artistry, through all the changes of life, right to the end." That was the question I asked myself one afternoon as I visited my trainer, Mr. Stairmaster, in the basement of our house.

While Stairmaster is torturing me, I sometimes disengage from the pain by looking at the pictures on the wall. My eyes turn toward the wedding pictures, my own (who is that kid, thinking he's old enough to get married?), my in-laws', and my parents'. My eyes settle on my parents' picture, and I begin to ponder their lives.

Their wedding anniversary was Christmas Day, which seems silly until you realize they were madly in love, WWII was happening, and Dad's only day off was December 25. So they married and hopped on the train back to the war, opening their suitcases along the way to find them filled with rice.

They look so happy, he in his military uniform, she in her wedding dress. They were filled with lavish hope that day. Both were optimists, enthusiasts, downright fun-loving people. In the family archives there's a record of Dad, who grew up in farm country, "borrowing" his friend's cow and tying it to the door of the courthouse, just for laughs. (And he was arrested for the stunt too, "just for laughs.") His sense of humor never left him. When I was young he bought fake vomit; he'd toss it on the ground at parties and laugh when people tried to rinse it off the cement. He bought a fake rubber hot dog once and watched as Mom felt it with disgust before tossing it in the garbage disposal, where it shot out like a rocket. She screamed, while Dad fell out of his chair laughing. He was usually laughing, at least from what I can remember.

Mom was a social butterfly in her college days, with a sense of humor that could leave you in stitches. Both of them studied to be teachers and then, right in the midst of it all, there was the war.

I look at Dad, in his uniform, and the picture nearly comes to life—it's like he's there with me. I get off the Stairmaster and, since nobody's home, decide now's a good time for a conversation. Wiping the sweat from my forehead, I look at him and speak: "Hi, Dad. I've been looking at your picture while working out. You and Mom looked so happy then, so hopeful, even there in the midst of the war. What were you hoping for?"

He's smiling at me, full of confidence, and somehow I'm not surprised when he responds, "I was in love, son. Your mom and I were going to build a life together, raise a family. But there was the war to be fought first, and unlike you, looking in the rearview mirror, we'd no idea how it would turn out. Still, you need to believe in the future and not get paralyzed by fear. So we assumed, or at least hoped, things would all work out, for the country, and for us. And of course, it did."

"But the war didn't treat you well. Mom told me you caught pneumonia several times."

"That's right. I don't know if it was the barracks, the cold, the food, the stress. I had the same disease often as a baby, and it weakened my resistance. Throw all those things in the mix, and I suppose it was inevitable. That's why I was sick so often when you were just a kid, why it was hard for me to play sports with you. God knows I wanted to, son, more than anything; I just couldn't."

"I didn't understand any of that when I was small. All I knew was that when I was out shooting hoops and you came home, you'd play H-O-R-S-E, but you couldn't play one-on-one, couldn't dribble or defend me. You'd try, and then you'd start wheezing and need to stop. You'd apologize and go inside. I was bummed you couldn't play. You were my best friend during junior high. Did you know that?" I wipe some tears from my eyes.

"Best friend? I doubt I was good at that. Being promoted from teacher, to principal, to superintendent takes a piece out of you—a big piece. I just didn't have the time, and with the bad lungs . . ."

"But when you came home, you played with me, even if it

was only for two minutes. I loved those two minutes." I look at the picture and remember the baskets we shot together, the baseball we played together. I assure him, "It wasn't much, but it was enough."

Dad changes the subject: "Things never turn out like you think they will. After the war, we got pregnant, your mom and I. But when the time came for the birth, there were complications. Mom nearly bled to death, and the baby died after a day. I can't describe the grief, and the terror of nearly losing your mom too." I try to imagine him comforting Mom, but there's no reference point, because nothing that awful happened to them during my years at home. Dad pressed the point. "You can't know how terrible it was. You've three kids of your own, each of them healthy, marvelous, beautiful."

This does me in, because at the birth of each of my children I felt the sting of his absence. I tell him of my pain. "But you never met them, Dad. You died too soon!" My eyes fill with tears again, as they did every time one of my children was born. "I wanted you to know them, wanted them to laugh at your stupid jokes, to hear you pray, to know how much you loved me, and how well." I'm crying now, full on, the sweat mixed with the salt water of tears.

"I know them, son."

I realize I've suddenly made this all about me. I apologize and return to Dad's grief.

He continues. "We buried our baby, and the doctor told your mom she could never have children. It was a bad week." He lets those words sink in. "But hope is a strong thing. We rebuilt. Your mother has a rich faith, a great capacity for hope. She went back to teaching and after a few years we started thinking about adoption. There's nothing she desired more than loving her family. God gave us your sister first. Four years later, he gave us you."

I remember a letter I have in my files. "I have the note you wrote to your mom when you brought me home. It was powerful to read about what a gift you thought I was, how much you loved me. I was too young when you died to tell you this, but maybe now I can say it—thanks for taking me in. I wouldn't have chosen anyone else in the world—really I wouldn't have."

I have questions about change, and these two seem to have handled boatloads of it with more grace than I could imagine. So I say, "I'm writing this book about the chance we each have to bring hope into the world, about being the artists God created us to be. You were a great artist, Dad. I have one of your drawings on the wall of my office. But you were great in the art of life too. I remember your funeral. Hundreds of people. Handel's *Messiah*—the 'Hallelujah Chorus.' Your friends telling me that your faith was real at work. I've *done* funerals since then, and I know this much: yours was remarkable. People knew they'd been blessed by knowing you. You painted hope on the world, even in the midst of your own pain and sickness. I struggle because I'm so easily done in by change and loss. How did you manage it?"

"I've always been a teacher and a leader, just like you," my dad told me.

I pause and consider whether, in the absence of knowing my genetic heritage, I didn't receive something even grander—the imprint of my adoptive dad.

"I was a teacher in college, on the track team, when I could run like the wind. I was a leader in war, as a sergeant for my platoon. I was a teacher in the classroom, and when they promoted me, I was a leader for the other teachers. I was your teacher too. You didn't think I was shooting baskets after a long day at work because I liked to play H-O-R-S-E, did you? That's when we talked. When my health left me completely and I couldn't leave the bed, you'd come in and we'd watch the World Series together, or college basketball. We talked then too. Thanks for that. I was still teaching, with you as my student, until the day I died."

I remember those moments sitting on the bed when the Oakland A's were in the World Series, talking about the girl I was thinking about dating, or the merits of a career in architecture. I remember those talks, even to his last days. It all makes sense looking back on it through the rearview mirror. That's why I still love the World Series, and college basketball. I thank him. Then I think of Mom.

"What about Mom? She lost the baby; then she lost you. Then she lost Sue, my sister, the daughter you adopted. She called me when I was teaching in Montana to tell me Sue died of a heart attack—at forty-three. She left four kids behind under the age of seventeen. All that loss. What was God thinking?"

I pause and look at Mom's face in the picture. An ocean of grief would roll over her in the decades after that wedding day, but on that day she knew nothing of it, smiling and ready to take on the world. "She's so alone now—but she seems at peace."

"She is alone, and she's suffered a lot." Dad pauses to make sure this next part sinks in. "And she's at peace. She prays for you, you know. Every time you call she tells you that. When she was young the world was her canvas, and she made her big part beautiful by painting acts of service to others on it. Her canvas is smaller now. She barely leaves her room. But she loves you. And she prays for you. That's her art. Her way of imparting beauty was always by serving, always by making others feel loved and cared for. It wasn't spectacular. It never made headlines or got published. But it was priceless. And now? Well, the fact is that the size of the canvas, the location of the canvas, the strokes we use to create our art, those things will change, but we'll always have the chance to be the artists we were created to be until the day we die, and beyond. We're born artists, son, all of us are. And when we find our craft, we should use it until the very end. Tell them that in your book."

I wipe a tear. "I will. I'll tell them you told me."

I pause and debate offering one last word before returning to the Stairmaster. "I could have used a few more conversations like this."

He smiles but doesn't respond. Maybe some questions are never answered. "I'll see you later," he says, as I'm startled awake.

THE CONTEXTS, THEY ARE A-CHANGIN'

Having fallen asleep on the sofa after my workout, I open my eyes. It was all a dream, but so true, so vivid, so real. Dad died in 1973; my sister in '95. It's been a long time, but grief and questions run deep, and these dreams help put the pieces together. I'm profoundly grateful for the example of my parents, who walked through the tumultuous waters of change and loss with enough honesty, courage, and grace to be a blessing to others. They weren't perfect people, of course. But they were, each of them in their own way, artists. Only retrospectively can I see clearly enough to realize each has been able to pour hope into the world, not just in spite of but even because of the changes and challenges they faced.

Dad reminded me in the dream that our gifts don't change; they're hardwired into who we are. "The gifts and calling of God are without repentance" is the way Paul said it.[3] "If you're a writer, write" is how Rainer Maria Rilke said it.

In every instance, the point's the same. Whether you're made to paint, cook, garden, or practice law, medicine, or hospitality, there is, behind that particular skill, a wiring that enables you to find meaning and joy in your craft and to bless others. It's what you're wired to do that is central, and my dad was reminding me that the wiring doesn't change with the context, even though the context does inevitably change.

For Dad this meant his calling wasn't to be a principal or schoolteacher; those were just contexts. His calling was teaching and leading, and that's something he'd do all of his days. For Mom it didn't mean being a mom to little kids or a caregiver to the elderly. Those were contexts. She was born to serve and she did this with children, a sick husband, the elderly, and people in the city of Fresno who needed to pay their water bill. It's how she's wired, no matter the context.

I sometimes think we've got it backwards. Thinking that the key to living a meaningful life has to do with the context, we agonize over the particulars of when and where and what: East Coast or West? Mountains or ocean? Teach in university or high school? Pastor a large church or house church? Single or married? How much ink is spent encouraging people to pursue particular contexts, as if the contexts are the key? We've found some certain context that we like, and over time we begin confusing the context with the calling.

This was exactly the problem my wife and I faced after the "prophet from India" predicted that God was calling us to a different context for ministry, that God was calling us to Seattle. We did not want to hear that because we like stars better than streetlights, and trees better than skyscrapers. Context was, we thought, a mission-critical piece to our calling. I traveled down to Seattle and met with people, telling them my contextual concerns, and they invited me anyway. Context, it turns out, is secondary at best. The important thing is being the artist you're made to be.

The fact is that contexts are changing all the time. Things break into our lives from the outside, or grow up from the inside, and happen. My daughter was downsized from schoolteaching in our city, due to the economy, so she now lives in Europe, where she'll continue to be an artisan of hope, still teaching English literature, but now to young people living in Germany, most of whom are children of missionaries. Other friends just moved back to the U.S. from Bolivia after serving there many years. Their art remains. Their context changes.

I called my mom Sunday night to talk with her. She's ninety now, and because we've always been a baseball family, I asked her if she'd been watching the Giants. "If they've been playing, I've been watching them," she said, and then added, "I just can't remember if they've been playing." Pictures flash through my mind of my mom and dad pulling me out of second grade because the Giants were coming to Fresno to play an exhibition game against the Cleveland Indians. We went, all of us, even skipping Wednesday night church, which made my mom feel like a sinner, but more of a true fan. Now she can't remember if she watched a game earlier in the day.

But she prays. "I'm praying for you, son. You're preaching too many times on Sunday. I'm praying that you'll be strong." It's her way of serving at ninety, and serving is what she's always done. What's more, I think if we could peel back the curtain, her prayers might just be a major factor in why, after fifteen years, I'm still doing what I do, because God knows I've never been good at perseverance until the last fourteen years. Thanks, Mom.

Nobody anticipates the contexts of tomorrow, but they matter less than we think—especially if we've been practicing our craft as artisans of hope faithfully, day after day, in the previous years and months.

13

ART IN THE GARDEN

So Sow . . .

To live for yourself alone, hoarding your life for your own sake,
is in almost every sense that matters to reduce your life to a life
hardly worth the living, and thus to lose it.

—Frederick Buechner

When the credits roll, we wonder what we did with our lives,
and what was the meaning.[1]

—Donald Miller

Walking through a forest is deceptive. To the casual stroller, it feels like a meander through a static place, because on most days nothing spectacular, or loud, or showy happens. You can even stop walking for a few seconds, and if you really pay attention you can hear something that's increasingly rare in our world: silence. The forest feels comfy, cozy, certain, static. It isn't.

I met a man once at a hot springs, high up in the Cascade Mountains, who'd been hiking the five-mile trail to visit this same place every summer for the past seventy years. He was eighty-four. I was intrigued that he always came to the same place, because I get bored easily and like to visit new spots all the time. When I asked him about it he said, "I don't come to the same place every year. This place is always changing. I see differences every time I'm up here. Look over there." He points out a tiny fir tree, maybe six inches high. "That was new last year, but the year before that it was a seed—growing and alive, but hidden. That's the way it is. There's always life happening up here, but a lot of it is tucked away. Most people don't see anything, because they're looking for big thrills, like seeing a bear." He points out lichen that's grown, branches that have fallen, nests that have been built or abandoned. "Bears are fine, but the real action is in the soil."

That's what Jesus said too:

> Behold, the sower went out to sow; and as he sowed,
> some seeds fell beside the road, and the birds came and
> ate them up. Others fell on the rocky places, where they
> did not have much soil; and immediately they sprang up,
> because they had no depth of soil. But when the sun had
> risen, they were scorched; and because they had no root,
> they withered away. Others fell among the thorns, and
> the thorns came up and choked them out. And others fell
> on the good soil and yielded a crop, some a hundredfold,
> some sixty, and some thirty. He who has ears, let him hear.[2]

This farming and gardening stuff is wholly unspectacular work, but both Jesus and the old man in the forest are on to something: in the midst of unspectacular familiarity, sown seeds are laying the foundation for big changes. It requires faith to drop some seeds in soil and then just wait. Cheering and checking on the health of the seed won't make it grow any faster. Neither will marketing campaigns or social networking programs. But seeds, faithfully sown, will find some good soil now and again, and the combination of good seed, good soil, and the Giver of Life is a winner. Fruit happens.

If we're to be artisans of faith we need to be weaned away from our addictions to the spectacular and realize instead that simply showing up, day after day, and creating splashes of beauty and grace will eventually bring fruit. I've been fortunate to encounter lots of gardener/artists in my time, and each one has taught me something about being an artisan of hope, as their seeds sown have germinated in lots of soils, including the soil of my own life. For instance . . .

JOAN THOMAS

The year was 1947. The place was the outskirts of a small village in the Lakes District of Northern England. A diminutive woman named Joan Thomas mills about with other Englanders as the auction is about to begin; she's here because of a vision for ministry that her husband, Ian, is carrying in his heart. Being both an evangelist and a major in the British army, Ian has a profound burden for sharing the liberating truth of what life in Christ really means. He'll tell his discovery to anyone willing to listen, but he has a particular burden for young adults.

Major Ian Thomas had taken up a relationship with Jesus as a child, then spent his teen years in a relentless cycle of frustration as he tried, and failed, to live faithfully for Christ. After years of struggle, he finally came to discover the liberating truth that he wasn't called to perform for Jesus but rather to learn how to let Christ, the master artist, express genuine life through him as he lived in a state of conscious dependency. He would later declare, "I learned to say, 'Lord Jesus, I can't, You never said I could; but You can, and always said You would. That is all I need to know.' From that moment life became the adventure that

God always intended it to be."[3] It was this particular message Major Thomas wanted to share with young people.

He'd recently seen something called a "conference center" where people gathered for rest, recreation, and study in the south of England. This was new in Great Britain, and the concept became a seed of vision. Major Thomas and his wife were conversing one day about the future, after the war, and he told her, "We'll need a large house." He wanted to establish a place where young people could come and discover the adventure of life in Christ for themselves; his wife has gone to a public auction to bid on a large estate, believing it could become the center of hospitality and teaching where this vision might become reality.

It's a glorious castle but in need of some work. Her businessman friend bids higher and higher on her behalf, until he reaches their agreed-upon limit, at which point he whispers, "What should I do?" and she says, "Just go a little bit higher." He offers one more bid. It's the final one, and the property is purchased with the vision of a Bible school being born.

World War II has just ended; Ian Thomas is still in Germany, working with the Allies in the army of occupation. German officials, knowing this British major, begin sending German youth to his castle with the goal of building reconciliation between the youth of England and Germany. The first thirty German students arrive for one month, and so it comes to pass that Capernwray Hall Bible School is born.

Donald Miller, in *A Million Miles in a Thousand Years*, writes, "I believe there is a writer outside ourselves, plotting a better story for us, interacting with us, even, and whispering a better story into our consciousness."[4] Why does a British major have a fire in his bones to share Jesus with young people, including those considered his enemy? The best answer is that God had put the seeds of this story in the soil of his heart. God was this "writer outside ourselves" with a grand story, a vision, a plot line. He gave this vision to Ian Thomas, who then responded by tossing a few seeds here and there to see how God's story might unfold. It unfolded in a castle, which became a Bible school, which eventually became twenty-seven Bible schools scattered like little seeds all around the world. All because a man listened for God's voice and his wife bid "a little bit higher."

ESTHER, HANNAH, AND JOHN

"Are we there yet?" is the mantra my sister and I repeat as we enter the redwood forest of the California coast. It's 1968, and I'm twelve. We're excited because this forest is where we go every summer for a week, and it's become our favorite place in the world. We're going to Grandma's house.

Grandma is a widow who lives with her sister in a cabin surrounded by enormous coastal redwoods. Both work as cooks for Mount Hermon, a Christian Bible center and camp. This little spot became an annual tradition because my dad is a schoolteacher, and staying with his mom, in such a beautiful spot, makes for a great budget vacation. My dad also has a vast love for his mom, and with good reason.

Love, grace, and hospitality bubble out of Grandma Esther and her sister, Hannah, naturally and relentlessly, like a mountain spring. We're greeted with huge hugs as soon as we get out of the car, and "There are fresh cookies and milk for you as soon as you unpack. I'm soooo glad you're here with us this week!" It's not an act, either; my sister and I *know* Grandma and Aunt Hannah love us, with a kind of knowing that comes from undeniable evidence at every turn. In the morning there will be fresh homemade cinnamon rolls, bacon and eggs, and orange juice. All week we'll eat like kings and queens because these two ladies are painting hope in the world by cooking for hundreds of people, and their culinary art continues off the clock, with us as the recipients. They have vast storehouses of joy and energy, especially since, seen through my young eyes, they are so very old.

As soon as I've eaten my cookies, I run to the place behind the cabin where there's a circle of redwoods, all of them old and huge. I lie down on the forest floor and look up at the shafts of light penetrating the canopies of branches, breathing deeply as the scent of redwood bathes me in a moment of "shalom." Though I don't know it yet, this place is preparing the soil of my heart for some seeds that will be planted there this week. I love this space—even at twelve, the quiet and the dance of light and shadow do something to my soul.

The mist of ocean fog hangs in the trees most summer mornings and evenings, mixing the aromas of salty seawater with sweet redwood sap and campfire smoke. It's cool, and this is a blessed contrast to the summer oven of the Central Valley, from which our family has briefly escaped. We joyfully break out sweaters to cover the chill of the evening. This is why the smell of woodsmoke, wet wool, and evergreens is still my favorite perfume. In this space, I feel embraced, safe, and hence, open.

At night I sometimes walk the short road from Grandma's house to the conference center where meetings are held for adults, because I like the music, and because this is where you can buy ice cream, after the evening's Bible talk ends. One evening I walk up to the center and sit in the back row as the meeting begins. When the singing is finished a man gets up and starts to speak. I like him immediately because his accent tells me he's not from here, so I stay and listen. His name is John Hunter, and he's here all the way from a Bible school in England to teach for the week and sow some seeds of good news for whoever will listen on the California coast.

His teaching is so clear that even at twelve, I get it, or at least enough of it to want more. He talks about "limiting God" and the fundamental theme, as I hear it through my middle-school brain, is that all of us have great things we're called to do, but choices we make get in the way and we end up limiting God, falling short of our potential.

The man even had a book by the same title as his sermon. I ran back to Grandma's and managed to talk my folks out of three dollars so I could buy my own copy. It was the first book I ever purchased and the first I read without pressure from schoolteachers. The rest of the week, I'd walk down to the creek that ran below Grandma's house, prop myself against a fallen log, and read Hunter's words with the sounds of a quiet stream as background music. I learned about how easily we limit God and how that limiting shrinks our life, shaping us into so much less than we could be if we'd let God have his way with us. Long before my life got hard, long before I sensed a calling to ministry, that summer gave me an encounter with reality, and I received some seeds of destiny through the spiritual farmer John Hunter.

Who's more important in that story: Hunter or Grandma? Sometimes we think that whatever it is we happen to do as faith art isn't "big enough" or "spiritual enough," but I'm telling you: the warmth and safety of Grandma's cabin was every bit as important in my encounter with God as the great Bible teacher from England. As much as I liked listening to him, that cabin and all it contained when I was a child created an atmosphere where I had the space to encounter eternal things. The Celtic church had a name for this: "thin places," where the distance between eternity and earth is permeable. My grandma and great-aunt made a thin place out of hugs, laughter, and cinnamon rolls.

By now I've married, had two children, and accidentally become a pastor on an island. I'm putting together a retreat for our church and am looking for a good speaker to come teach our flock. However, living in isolation as I am, and being a nondenominational church as we are, I don't know of any good Bible teachers who will come and speak to a group as small as ours.

I still have *Limiting God* on my shelf, twenty years after hearing John Hunter at Mount Hermon. From the back of the book, I know that this man had become friends with Ian Thomas and, as a result of the major's influence and invitation, had begun teaching the Bible at Capernwray Hall while spending his summers preaching at conferences in the United States. Over the years I'd known a few people who'd spent a year at the English castle and had their lives changed, profoundly, for the better. *It would be incredible,* I think, *to find someone from that Capernwray community to come and speak to our tiny church,* but what are the odds? England is a long way from our little island, and even if it weren't, there will only be forty or fifty of us at the retreat. That feels like a small number for any really good Bible teacher to spend time with, and we can't pay much.

I'm talking one day to one of our members, a woman who lived in a tree house for a little while. She'd just recently started up with Jesus, and I'd baptized her in the ocean on a cold, stormy day in a "No Devils" T-shirt while howling wind created whitecaps in the tidewaters. I'm telling her about my plans to have a retreat, and how I'd like to find someone from Torchbearers to come talk to us.

She smiles; turns out she's been thinking about attending Bible school and knows what's nearby. "They have a sister school in Canada now. It's only about a hundred miles north of here, on another island." I call the school and the director answers the phone himself. When I invite him to speak to our church retreat, he accepts immediately.

A friend of mine flies me to Canada to pick him up, and then we drive up to the camp in the Cascade Mountains, where he speaks to us for the weekend. His messages hit home, reminding me of John Hunter. His name is Charlie, and he attended Capernwray Hall Bible School in England and *knew* John Hunter, the man who'd introduced me to Jesus in a real way when I was twelve.

Charlie and I spend the weekend talking theology and become fast friends. He's ten years older and, though I don't know it that weekend, will become a friend and mentor for the next twenty years. We'll teach together all over Canada, and other places too. That fall he brings students down to stay with me at the island church so I can teach them for a week. Soon I'm going up to Canada, teaching at Capernwray Harbour Bible School on Thetis Island. During one of my stays there I meet Major Ian Thomas in person, and he invites me to speak in England, in the castle that is Capernwray Hall Bible School.

When I was in England for the conference and just about to speak, I was sitting near the front, nervously going over my notes. After all, the people here were all leaders and staff members of the Torchbearer Bible Schools, and in a sense my spiritual roots go back there because of John Hunter. However, a friend interrupted me and said, "Richard, I'd like you to meet someone, a good friend of mine." There, standing in front of me, was John Hunter.

He held out his hand, but like a typical Californian I hugged him, overwhelmed with gratitude for the gift of meeting the one who'd sown seeds in my heart. I told him about how much he'd impacted me when I was twelve, sitting in the back of the meeting hall in the midst of the forest, and would have been embarrassed by the tears in my eyes except that he had tears of his own as he said, "Now it's your turn to sow seeds. I'm looking forward to hearing you." When I began teaching that evening, I saw him sitting near the back, his Bible open, pen in hand, the same way I was listening to him twenty years earlier. That's the way it is with sowing seeds. You drop them here and there along the way, and sometimes you don't realize the impact you're having. That's okay because the joy is in the sowing, not the reaping, or at least that's the way it's supposed to work.

Because of all the seeds that had been sown in my life by people baking cinnamon rolls, bidding on castles, flying from England to teach in California, plus a tugboat worker's knowledge and the willingness of a Bible school director to come and spend time at a tiny church without consideration of money, I was able to sow seeds by teaching the Bible in England and, later, Austria, Germany, Central America, and farther corners of the world. *Who knows what will happen when we get into farming?*

PASTOR SINGH

It was while I was teaching for the Torchbearers ministry in India, twenty-five years after listening to John Hunter, that a pastor there sowed seeds in my life regarding my calling to become a pastor in Seattle. There'd been political tensions in the city where the school was located, so my friend Satish suggested I leave a day or two early. He arranged for me to make my way back to New Delhi, where I'd stay with a friend of his until the time of my flight. A night train later I was in a cab, careening through utterly foreign streets, as the driver made his way to the scribbled address I'd handed him.

Thus it was that I ended up staying with a hospitable Delhi pastor. The next morning we were sitting together eating eggs and rice, talking about Hinduism, Christianity, Delhi, and his calling to ministry. He told me he'd been a missionary for years, supported by a church in Seattle. When I asked him which church, he took another bite before saying, "Bethany Community Church; perhaps you've heard of it?"

I told him that, indeed, I'd not only heard of it, but I went there as a college student, and that the only sermon I remember was the one given by its pastor when he'd returned from India. He'd read from his journal and had to stop reading, having been moved to tears by what he'd seen, both the beauty and the tragedy. "You don't forget a sermon like that one," I continued. "Did you know Pastor John?" I asked.

"He was sitting right where you are now," the man said. Then he stopped eating his eggs, put down his fork, and spoke directly and dramatically: "God wants you to be the pastor of Bethany Community Church."

I laughed. I told him that if God had this in mind for me he'd tell me directly, and that I'd missed the memo, at least until now.

"Don't forget this conversation," he said. I assured him I wouldn't, but promptly did, being utterly content with my calling to live in the mountains, travel, and teach.

That conversation was in 1993. The seeds my Indian friend planted would germinate in December 1995, when my wife and I left the comfort of our ministry in the mountains to move to the city. Since then, I've been privileged to be part of a tremendous community filled with artisans and gardeners of hope who've been flung out around the globe to sow their seeds and paint their pictures. University students, doctors, nurses, software and airplane engineers, moms, dads, literal artists and gardeners, entrepreneurs—they're sowing the seeds of hope in thousands of ways.

SO SOW

Telling my story the way I have is risky because reading it is almost like looking at a spiritualized ESPN highlight reel of yesterday's greatest shots. We see a spectacular jumper at the buzzer, or the sinking of a thirty-foot putt, and think, *Yes! This is what it's all about.* Thrilled by the prospect of starting a Bible school or baking life-changing cinnamon rolls, we jump in with both feet, eager to impart blessing in our world.

But, as the saying goes, "The journey of a thousand miles always begins with one step," it's also true that the first step is usually easier than step number 12,357. In our journey to become artisans of hope, mostly unspectacular moments fill our days. While it's important to get our bearings and find our unique sense of calling (as I discussed in chapter 9), it's even more important to recognize that most days are filled with neither major setbacks nor visible gains. Most days, plants look the same as yesterday, and so do paintings, children, orphanages, AIDS clinics, churches, and relationships.

This "sameness" factor can be discouraging in a culture raised on highlight reels, and for this reason, lots of people lose sight of their calling as artists. Though the beginning is exciting, tomorrow eventually becomes achingly similar to yesterday, and artists decide they need a better high than what Eugene H. Peterson calls "a long obedience in the same direction." So, whether it happens slowly or overnight, there are always some who drop out along the way. "You've lost your first love" is how Jesus expressed it to a certain church once.

How can we continue to sow seeds, continue to perfect our craft, day after familiar day? The author of the letter to the Hebrews said, "You have need of endurance,"[5] and he wasn't only talking about fires and financial meltdowns. More than anything else, I think he was talking about sameness and the very real dangers of boredom.

The good artists, though, have learned to be less concerned with seeing the fruits of their sowing and more concerned with the sowing itself. They've become people who take delight in doing what they do, rather than in the rewards that may or may not come from doing what they do. Good artists enjoy each brushstroke even though few of them will ever create masterpieces. Good teachers enjoy each interaction with students even though few of them will be indelibly life-changing. For others the joy comes in providing hospitality, or throwing a party, or doing heart surgery. But regardless, for the real artists, the joy comes in the craft itself, rather than worrying about the fruit that will come from the craft.

After Hurricane Katrina, our Seattle Symphony put on a benefit fund-raiser, and a cellist was the evening's soloist. Lynn Harrell no doubt had done this a thousand times over the course of his career. He has, after all, played numerous times with every major orchestra in the world and made dozens of recordings. My wife and I had seats so close to the front you could see his eyes as he sat down to play Fauré's "Élégie." With each stroke of the bow, this man was wholly present, drawing pathos and energy from his instrument and sharing it with us, so that we might share freely with hurricane victims. What struck me most profoundly that night, in watching Mr. Harrell, was that there were no casual notes in his repertoire. Every tone received his full heart; everything mattered; every note was rife with the possibility of great joy.

Later that night, as I lay in bed replaying his performance in my mind, I thought about how this same "wholeheartedness" was present in all the people I respected. There were no insignificant meals for Grandma; no insignificant brushstrokes for Juliette, no insignificant Bible sessions for John Hunter. I'm privileged to have seen dozens of people go before me who lived out their days as artisans of hope—not perfectly, but faithfully—right up to the end because their joy was found not in being famous or impactful or even in seeing the fruit of their labors. Rather, the joy was found in the doing of the thing—faithfully carrying out each brushstroke for the love of God.

This is liberating, energizing; this is the one consistent quality I've found in every great artist.

The old preacher from chair 8 understood this when he wrote: "*Whatever your hand finds to do, do it with all your might, for in the grave, where you are going, there is neither working nor planning, nor knowledge nor wisdom.*"[6] This is the day to sow seeds, however small or big they may seem, of hope in the garden of the world, lavishly, creatively, joyfully. What are you waiting for?

EPILOGUE

Six AM: The sunrise is achingly beautiful this morning as I take my coffee outside, in the midst of a fir forest. Mist rises from the ground while the sky brightens to a stunning blue, its hues brightening from east to west. I can see my breath and the birds begin to sing, first one, then two, and then quickly a symphony, cacophonic yet perfectly harmonized.

I love May in the mountains. This past week, while I've been focused on writing, I've known two intense thunderstorms. I've also gone higher one afternoon for the solitude of backcountry skiing as snow dusted the peaks, and up there I carved turns on steep uncharted powder. It's all so perfect that I don't want to leave. I feel like Peter as I talk with Jesus over my morning coffee: "Couldn't we just stay here, you and me? I'll bring the family up here and we'll just inhale the glory of creation. We'll love you and care for the earth. It's enough, right?"

I imagine Jesus laughing and shaking his head, pointing south toward Seattle as he says, "You know where you belong.

Better pack the car." I know that when I arrive home this afternoon I will step back into the midst of a very full life. Within the church I lead there are people newly unemployed. Someone's cancer has returned. A marriage is hanging by a thread, and some people are feeling stuck between the mountains of raising children and caring for aging parents. On top of it, we're adding staff and making big decisions because our church seems to have run out of room on Sunday mornings, and we're trying to more effectively love and serve a very needy part of our city. It's all a bit much for me, and though I love it, I don't feel like I have what it takes, don't feel like I have the wit, wisdom, charisma, or leadership ability.

I tell Jesus this and he agrees. "That's right, man—you *don't* have what it takes." Then he quickly adds, "But you do have what you need."

Why is Jesus talking like this, in contradictions? He drives me crazy sometimes with his talking about losing life to find it, and the first being last; and now this. "What do I need?" I ask, and he reminds me: the bread and the wine.

He's right. I think about the many times I've done weddings and how, when the mic is off, I serve communion to the couple. I give them each a piece of bread and remind them that this represents the body of Christ, and that as bread, it represents both strength and satisfaction, because that's what bread does for you. I tell them that the best strength and satisfaction will be found not in each other or in any other relationship or endeavor, but in Christ. Then, with a wink, I say, "Remember, you are what you eat. Feast on Christ, friends, and find the strength to be all that you could never be on your own." Every time I say it, I get teary because of how much I ache for this couple to live larger, more honestly, joyfully, and generously than even they can imagine.

Then I give them the cup and I say, "Whatever grand ideals

you have for your marriage, I promise you this, you will fail." I know this because of my own failures, over and over again so often that they no longer surprise me. "The important thing, though, isn't that you fail; what matters is what you do after you fail. The cup represents forgiveness—the cup means you don't need to give up on the ideal. Jesus said it's the cup of his blood, shed for the forgiveness of sins, which is just another way of saying that our failures are covered, and every day we can have a fresh start—with God, and with each other. It's only because of this that your home will become a safe and beautiful place for truth-telling, intimacy, and hope."

Then I pause, and get a little teary again because I know, in the depths of my heart, how important this has been to me and I want it to be the same for them—liberating and transformative. "This is very good news, friends," I say to them. "It's better news than you know right now. Don't forget the cup."

These words are for me this morning as I finish my coffee, and I know that I need to meet with Jesus, need to appropriate once again the strength and forgiveness to continue my work back in the city. I pray, and when I'm finished I can almost hear Jesus talking . . . "It's time to pack the car. I've got the paint. You've got the brushes. There's some canvas in the city waiting for you. Let's go."

I get in the car, wave good-bye to the mountains, and start the engine.

NOTES

Introduction

1. Ecclesiastes 1:2–3 THE MESSAGE

Part One: Vision

1. Ephesians 2:10 THE MESSAGE

Chapter 1: Faith Art

1. Steven Pressfield, *The War of Art* (Boston: Grand Central Publishing, 2003), 26.

2. James 1:22 speaks of the necessity that we be "doers" of the word and not "hearers only" (NKJV). He goes on to speak of "only hearing" as a deception, similar, I believe, to the way we feel more fit and athletic after watching a sporting event on TV!

3. See Ephesians 2:10.

4. For example, see Matthew 10:8.

5. It's clear from the example of Jesus' life that studying the Bible and knowing its contents is a vital part of being equipped for God's purposes in our lives. It's also equally clear from passages like John 5:39 and Acts 13:27 that studying the Bible doesn't, in itself, lead to maturity and living well. We need to see both the importance and danger of studying the Bible, and it's this latter piece that's been lacking for too long.

6. The emergent church throws stones at the established church. The established

churches throw stones at the emergent church, and at each other. Christians fight over the meaning of communion, the return of Jesus, the nature of Jesus' kingdom, and the role of women in ministry, and on and on. But we're conspicuously silent when it comes to the more obvious matters of addressing materialism, human trafficking, environmental degradation, tribalism, and so on.

7. The *Book of Eli* movie is a study in how the same words can be used as a tool for both oppression and liberation. A good discussion guide can be found here: Craig Detweiler, Conversant Life, January 14, 2010, www.conversantlife .com/film/the-book-of-eli-soul-power.

8. On a recent teaching trip to Germany I made a little movie about someone who actively resisted the spiritual consumerism and passivity that was so rampant during the reign of Hitler. You can see it here: www.youtube.com/ watch?v=RAU1jK1n1wI.

Chapter 2: Canvas

1. See Genesis 27.

2. Luke 7:44 NIV

3. See Luke 7:39.

4. See Matthew 20:29–33.

5. You can read about them in Acts 13:27.

6. See Acts 17:16–34.

Chapter 3: Subject Matters

1. From Philip Yancey, *Soul Survivor* (Colorado Springs: WaterBrook, 2003).

2. Ecclesiastes 3:11 NIV

3. The terms "kingdom of heaven" or "kingdom of God" are used eighty-two times in the Gospels by Jesus and John the Baptist. Jesus generally focused on inviting people to change allegiances, from the kingdoms of this world to God's good reign, as the starting point of the good news.

4. Isaiah 2:2–4

5. Isaiah 9:6–7: "And His name will be called Wonderful Counselor, Mighty God, Eternal Father, Prince of Peace. There will be no end to the increase of His government or of peace."

6. See Isaiah 11:6–9.

7. See Romans 8:19–22.

8. Isaiah 65:21–22

9. My off-the-cuff interpretation of Matthew 13.

10. The biggest problem with this line of thinking is that when the church was at its finest, in its earliest days, before creeds, buildings, denominations, or political structures, *God was adding to their number daily* (see Acts 2:47). If the church at its healthiest is usually growing, we should at least ask a few questions if people are fleeing.

Chapter 4: Own or Rent

1. N. T. Wright, *Surprised by Hope* (New York: HarperOne, 2008), 193.
2. 1 Timothy 1:15
3. Acts 4:12 NKJV
4. Matthew 11:28 calls weary travelers to find rest, first of all, by coming to Christ.
5. 1 John 2:15
6. Colossians 3:2
7. Psalm 24:1
8. Romans 8:17
9. Hebrews 2:11 NIV
10. Matthew 5:5 NIV
11. See 1 John 2:16.
12. 1 John 5:19
13. See 2 Peter 3:10.
14. See Revelation 21:5
15. Matthew 13 contains both of these metaphors, describing the kingdom as present now, in small but profound ways.
16. See Revelation 21:6 *GW Translation*.
17. John 8:11 NLT
18. Matthew 10:8 NIV
19. Paul makes a clear distinction in Romans 5:10 between reconciliation and salvation. Reconciliation has to do with being made right with God, leaving the clear implication that salvation is larger in scope, having also to do with the transformation that enables us to live as the people of God, displaying Christ's character through our daily actions and relationships.
20. www.spillinghope.org

Part Two: The Primary Colors

1. Micah 6:8

Chapter 5: Do Justice

1. From THE MESSAGE
2. American Anti-Slavery Group, www.iabolish.org/slavery_today/country _reports/th.html.
3. Richard Stearns, president of World Vision, addresses justice issues globally in his book *The Hole in Our Gospel* (Nashville: Thomas Nelson, 2009).
4. See Isaiah 1:13.
5. See Isaiah 58.

6. Luke 4:18–19 (quoting from Isaiah 61:1–2)

7. Luke 4:21

8. Matthew 25:34–37 NIV

9. Dr. King would write, from a Birmingham jail, "When I was suddenly cata-pulted into the leadership of the bus protest in Montgomery, Alabama, a few years ago, I felt we would be supported by the white church, felt that the white ministers, priests and rabbis of the South would be among our strongest allies. Instead, some have been outright opponents, refusing to understand the freedom movement and misrepresenting its leader." K. Zirkel, Bates College, January 12, 2001, http://abacus.bates.edu/admin/offices/dos/mlk/letter.html.

10. See Brian D. McLaren, A New Kind of Christianity (San Francisco: Harper-One, 2010), 71–76 for a discussion of how the church opposed the abolition of slavery.

11. "When evangelical Christians were asked whether they would be willing to donate money to help children orphaned by AIDS, assuming they were asked by a reputable Christian organization that was doing this work, 3% said they would definitely help, while 52% said that they probably or definitely would not help." Stearns, The Hole in Our Gospel, 196–197.

12. David P. Gushee, "Remembering Rwanda," The Christian Century, April 20, 2004, www.religion-online.org/showarticle.asp?title=3048.

13. See Amos 5:23.

14. See James 1:27.

15. Jesus does set our hearts free from the slavery of sin. According to 1 Corin-thians 10, the exodus of the Jews from Egypt is a metaphor for what it means to be delivered by Christ and to follow him. It's also true that Exodus touches on physical oppression, because the trajectory of God's good reign on this earth will spell the end of oppression in all its forms, including slavery.

16. Isaiah 1:15

17. See Isaiah 1:16–17.

18. The Mentoring Project, www.thementoringproject.org/.

19. I.N. Network, February 25, 2010, www.innetworkusa.org/index.php?option =com_content&task=view&id=39&Itemid=45.

20. Walter's work is addressing human trafficking on two fronts. Systemically, he is at the forefront of changing laws so that the system no longer favors perpetrators. On a personal level, he's building relationships with priests, getting women freed, and helping them overcome the mountains of soul and body issues created by their horrific experience.

Chapter 6: Mercy Mountaineers

1. Matthew 10:8 NIV

2. See Genesis 12:1–3.

3. David Gushee writes that 90% of the country were self-proclaimed Christians.

David P. Gushee, "Remembering Rwanda," *The Christian Century*, April 20, 2004, www.religion-online.org/showarticle.asp?title=3048.

4. In Lisa Barnes Lapman and Michelle D. Shattuck, *God and the Victim: Theological Reflections on Evil, Victimization, Justice, and Forgiveness* (Grand Rapids, MI: Eerdmans, 1999), 132.

5. Catherine Claire Larson, *As We Forgive* (Grand Rapids, MI: Zondervan, 2009), 19.

6. Matthew 6:12

7. Jeremiah 6:14

8. See John 1:14.

9. In Larson, *As We Forgive*, 124.

10. Ibid, 37.

11. *As We Forgive*. A Laura Waters Hinson film; Stephen McEveety, executive producer.

12. Isaiah 53 expresses the truth that, because Christ has absorbed all wrath for all the sins of humanity, we've no wrath or vengeance to hand out. But we can also rest assured that forgiveness and its healing power only become real to the truly repentant, those who see that they've made destructive choices. The others, who live in denial, will surely suffer the consequences of holding on to their selfishness, for whatever form it takes, it will become a fire for them. You can learn more about this by listening to my teaching about hell at www.churchbcc.org.

13. See Donald B. Kraybill, Steven M. Nolt, and David L. Weaver, *Amish Grace: How Forgiveness Transcended Tragedy* (San Francisco: Jossey-Bass, 2010). An inspiring resource that will help you on toward your own freedom. I try to learn from the best in all areas—art from artists, climbing from climbers, and forgiveness from the Amish.

Chapter 7: Intimacy

1. Lyrics from Sufjan Stevens, "Vito's Ordination Song," *Greetings From Michigan*. Asthmatic Kitty, 2003.

2. John 1:14

3. Throughout this chapter I'll be talking about "walking with Jesus" and "walking with God" synonymously because, as John 1:14 and so many other biblical passages tell us, Jesus is God in human form. This might be elementary for some, but it ought to be earth-shattering news for all. God has lived as a man, so we can walk with God!

4. See Matthew 5:23–24.

5. See Matthew 5:27–28.

6. See Matthew 5:38–42.

7. Genesis 9 says all of us are created in the image of God. Because of this, moments of beauty and glory will break through in nearly everyone at times, in surprising places and ways.

8. John 15:4 NIV

9. Ephesians 5:31–32

10. Torchbearers International, www.torchbearers.org/about/history

11. Hebrews 12:2

12. Though it's well beyond the scope of this book, resources on my website illustrate the notion of "substitution" as it applies to salvation. I encourage you to read it at: www.thecolorsofhope.com.

13. Colossians 1:27 moves us beyond example, when Paul declares that the mystery of the ages is this: Christ lives in you—and this is the hope of God's glory being seen.

14. Jesus said, "By this all men will know that you are My disciples, if you have love for one another" (John 13:35), and he uses a particular Greek word for love—*agape*—in order to express that this love needs to pour from the very spirit and life of God within you.

Chapter 8: Pastel Fantasy

1. Job 2:10

2. See Hebrews 11.

3. Deuteronomy 28:1–6

4. 2 Corinthians 11:25, 27

5. For more on the life of this remarkable woman, and the White Rose resistance movement of Germany youth during WWII, please see the movie *Sophie Scholl—The Final Days*.

6. See Hebrews 6:19.

7. Attributed to Julian of Norwich.

8. See Ecclesiastes 3.

Chapter 9: The Artist's Identity

1. Ephesians 5 is one of the places where Paul unpacks the mysterious doctrine that Christ's followers are his bride. Our intimate receptivity and response will lead to a mysterious union that, just like human marriage, results in both great joy and fruitfulness.

2. Proverbs 3:5, emphasis added.

3. Psalm 73:25

4. Hebrews 11:6

5. N. T. Wright, *Surprised by Hope* (San Francisco: HarperOne, reprint edition, 2008), 208.

Chapter 10: Overcoming Failure

1. 2 Corinthians 3:5

2. Romans 7:24 ESV

3. See Genesis 38.

4. Richard Dahlstrom, O_2: *Breathing New Life Into Faith* (Eugene, OR: Harvest House, 2008).

5. Matthew 7:9–11

Chapter 11: Obstacles and Resistance

1. From Steven Pressfield, *The War of Art* (Boston: Grand Central Publishing, 2003).

2. John 1:29

3. Haggai 1:2

Chapter 12: Change

1. From Lynn Hall, *Where Have All the Tigers Gone?* (New York: Atheneum, 1989).

2. Ecclesiastes 1:4, 9, 11

3. Romans 11:29 KJV

Chapter 13: Art in the Garden

1. Donald Miller, *A Million Miles in a Thousand Years* (Nashville: Thomas Nelson, 2009), 122.

2. Matthew 13:3–9

3. See V. Raymond Edman, *They Found the Secret* (Grand Rapids, MI: Zondervan, 1984) for further development of Major Thomas's story.

4. Miller, 86.

5. Hebrews 10:36

6. Ecclesiastes 9:10 NIV

RICHARD DAHLSTROM's passion is to help people live in such a way that God's good reign is made visible in this broken and beautiful world. His ministry contexts include teaching at Bible schools around the world through Torchbearers Missionary Fellowship and speaking at conferences in North America.

Richard is the primary teaching pastor of Bethany Community Church in Seattle, a church founded in 1916 that's overflowing with young people painting the colors of hope through myriad creative ministries (see www.churchbcc.org). He's also been a pastor on a remote island and directed a Bible-based outdoor ministry in the Cascade Mountains. His first book, O_2: *Breathing New Life into Faith*, was picked as one of *Publishers Weekly*'s Top Ten Religious Books of 2008.

Richard's speaking schedule, free downloads, and musings about how faith changes everything can be found at www.richarddahlstrom.com. A study guide for *The Colors of Hope* can also be found at this site.

Richard finds relaxation in being outside, climbing up and skiing down mountains, enjoying food with family and friends, or simply reading a good book alone. He and his wife, Donna, still gather for a weekly lunch with their adult children, though the oldest can only be there via Skype, as she's a teacher in Europe.